SCOTLAND
FROM THE RAILS

MARY EVANS PICTURE LIBRARY

BENEDICT LE VAY

EDITION 1
BRADT TRAVEL GUIDES LTD, UK
THE GLOBE PEQUOT PRESS INC, USA

Bradt GUIDES

ABOUT THE AUTHOR

Benedict le Vay says he loves train travel because it's romantic, fun, comfortable, civilised, sociable, fascinating and doesn't damage the wonderful places you go to. To date, he has written five books for Bradt (many on the 'Eccentric Britain' theme) as well as holding down a full-time job as a Fleet Street newspaper sub-editor. He ascribes his early interest in railways to the fact that his mother grew up on his grandfather's private train, as the chief inspector of Indian Railways. Later, as a London schoolboy, he played cricket next to the tracks where the luxury *Golden Arrow* train to Paris steamed past. Needless to say, he dropped a few catches...

First edition February 2021
Reprinted July 2021
Bradt Travel Guides Ltd
31a High Street, Chesham, Buckinghamshire, HP5 1BW, England
www.bradtguides.com
Print edition published in the USA by The Globe Pequot Press Inc, PO Box 480, Guilford, Connecticut 06437-0480

Text copyright © 2021 Benedict le Vay
Maps copyright © 2021 Bradt Travel Guides Ltd
Photographs copyright © 2021 Individual photographers
Project Manager: Laura Pidgley

ISBN: 978 1 78477 762 3

British Library Cataloguing in Publication Data
A catalogue record for this book is available from the British Library

Front cover illustration Neil Gower (www.neilgower.com)
Design and maps Pepi Bluck, Perfect Picture and Ian Spick, Bradt Travel Guides
Typeset by Pepi Bluck, Perfect Picture and Ian Spick, Bradt Travel Guides
Production managed by Zenith Media; printed in the UK
Digital conversion by www.dataworks.co.in

Acknowledgements

My thanks go to Andrew Gurney, Bill Smith, Robin Popham, Chris and Judy Williams, Ed Bethune, Gavin Steele, Karen Watson and Chris Milburn. Thanks also go to the brilliant designer Pepi Bluck at Perfect Picture, Neil Gower for the front cover illustration and the team at Bradt, in particular Laura Pidgley, who have worked so hard to get this complicated book right. Any mistakes, however, are all my own. I know how picky railway fans are about history (and also how very sincerely they tell you something that clearly was never true). There will, I am sure, be points to put straight (no pun intended), suggestions and elaborations. Please write and let me know for future editions. Meanwhile, HAPPY WINDOW-GAZING.

DEDICATION TO THE
GREAT RAILWAYMEN AND WOMEN
OF SCOTLAND

Not just the famed greats like Kilmarnock-born Patrick Stirling, Edinburgh's genius Nigel Gresley and Alan Pegler. The forgotten hundreds who died building difficult tunnels, the Forth Bridge and other massive monuments to engineers' visions, whose lives were cheap, and names usually unrecorded. The navvies whose sweat and cusses and blisters built the deep cuttings and huge embankments by hand, creating a new wonder of the world. The ordinary men and women who kept it all running through world wars, under the Blitz's bombs and blackout. Who dug the trains out of snowdrifts for weeks in 1947 and 1963, often only to have the branch lines ripped up the next year. Whose backbreaking labour shovelling tons of coal into fireboxes got heavy trains over the summits. Whose professional dedication through long hours in lonely signalboxes got millions of us safely home billions of times. Who hacked out old sleepers and replaced rusted rails through the night at Christmas, while the rest of us feasted – or moaned about the railways. Who kept going through heartbreaking closures, cutbacks and botched reorganisations when interfering governments, stupid trade unions and the cynical travelling public seemed to be giving up. They carried on, waiting for the day when people would return to the rails, as they now have in droves, in numbers never seen before in peacetime, bigger even than when the network was a third larger.

THANKS. IT REALLY WAS ALL WORTH IT.

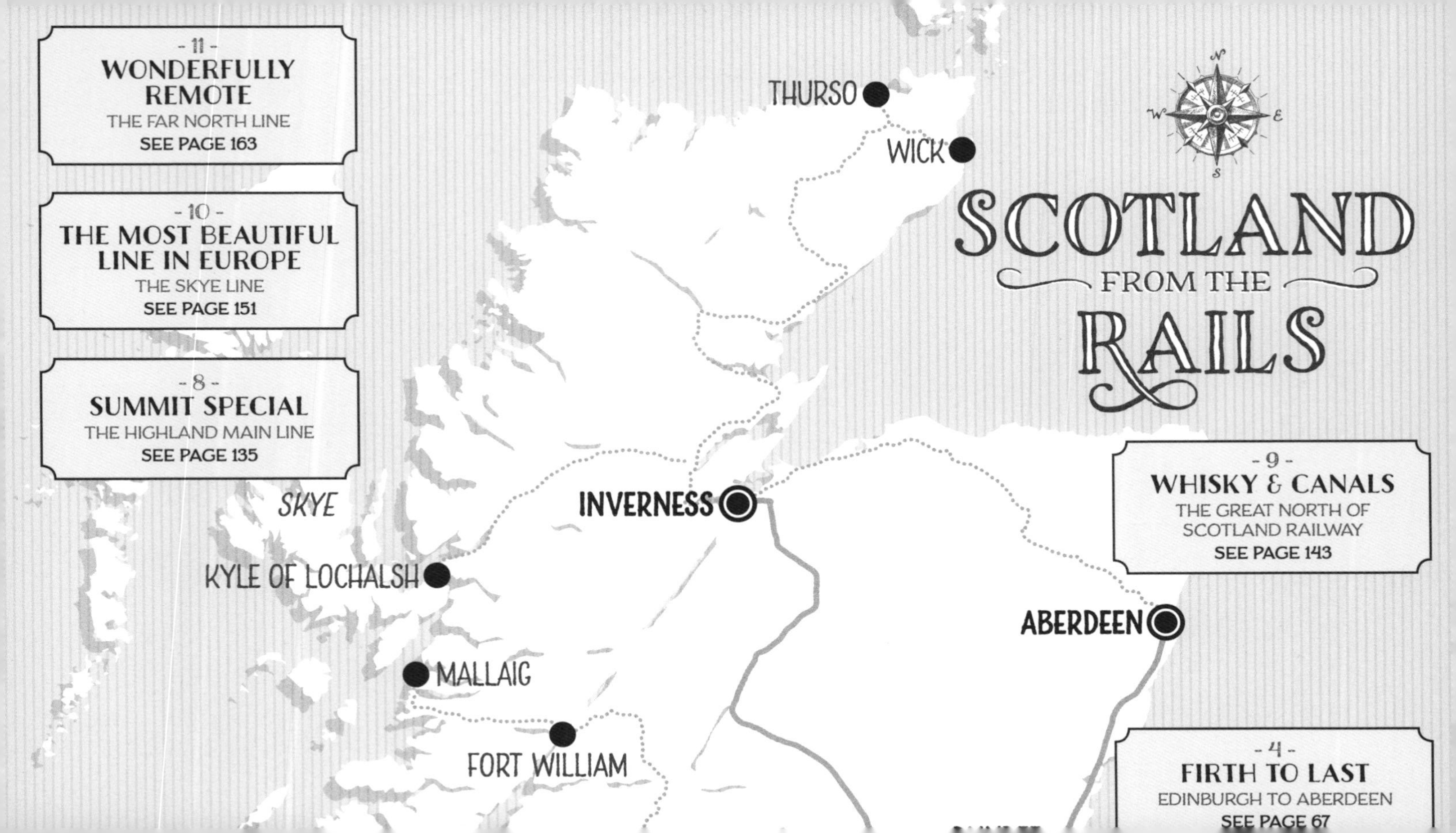

SCOTLAND
FROM THE
RAILS
N
E
S
W
- 11 -
WONDERFULLY REMOTE
THE FAR NORTH LINE
SEE PAGE 163
- 10 -
THE MOST BEAUTIFUL LINE IN EUROPE
THE SKYE LINE
SEE PAGE 151
- 8 -
SUMMIT SPECIAL
THE HIGHLAND MAIN LINE
SEE PAGE 135
- 9 -
WHISKY & CANALS
THE GREAT NORTH OF SCOTLAND RAILWAY
SEE PAGE 143
- 4 -
FIRTH TO LAST
EDINBURGH TO ABERDEEN
SEE PAGE 67
THURSO
WICK
INVERNESS
SKYE
KYLE OF LOCHALSH
MALLAIG
FORT WILLIAM
ABERDEEN

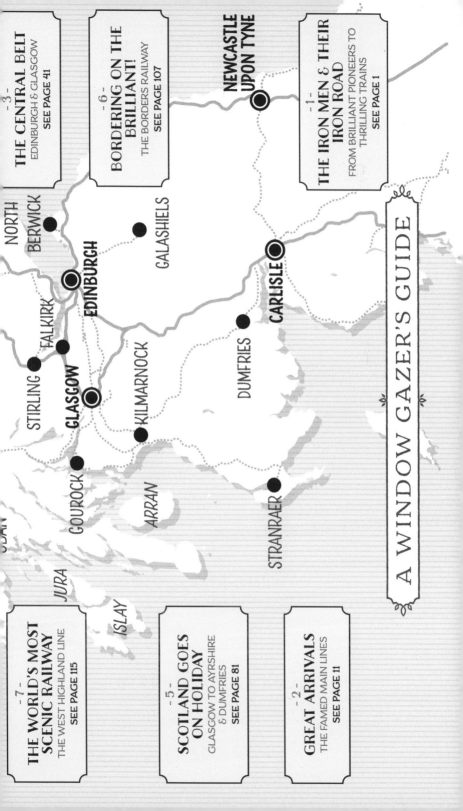

A WINDOW GAZER'S GUIDE

- 3 -
THE CENTRAL BELT
EDINBURGH & GLASGOW
SEE PAGE 41

- 6 -
BORDERING ON THE BRILLIANT!
THE BORDERS RAILWAY
SEE PAGE 107

NEWCASTLE UPON TYNE

- 1 -
THE IRON MEN & THEIR IRON ROAD
FROM BRILLIANT PIONEERS TO THRILLING TRAINS
SEE PAGE 1

NORTH BERWICK

GALASHIELS

EDINBURGH

FALKIRK

STIRLING

CARLISLE

GLASGOW

KILMARNOCK

DUMFRIES

GOUROCK

ARRAN

STRANRAER

JURA

ISLAY

- 7 -
THE WORLD'S MOST SCENIC RAILWAY
THE WEST HIGHLAND LINE
SEE PAGE 115

- 5 -
SCOTLAND GOES ON HOLIDAY
GLASGOW TO AYRSHIRE & DUMFRIES
SEE PAGE 81

- 2 -
GREAT ARRIVALS
THE FAMED MAIN LINES
SEE PAGE 11

CONTENTS

-6-
BORDERING ON THE BRILLIANT!
THE BORDERS RAILWAY   107

-7-
THE WORLD'S MOST SCENIC RAILWAY
THE WEST HIGHLAND LINE   115

-8-
SUMMIT SPECIAL
THE HIGHLAND MAIN LINE   135

-9-
WHISKY & CANALS
THE GREAT NORTH OF SCOTLAND RAILWAY   143

-10-
THE MOST BEAUTIFUL LINE IN EUROPE
THE SKYE LINE   151

-11-
WONDERFULLY REMOTE
THE FAR NORTH LINE   163

EDINBURGH WAVERLEY STATION

NETWORK RAIL

FEEDBACK REQUEST & UPDATES WEBSITE

At Bradt Travel Guides we're aware that guidebooks start to go out of date on the day they're published — and that you, our readers, are out there in the field doing research of your own. Contact us on ☎ 01753 893444 or ✉ info@bradtguides.com. We will forward emails to the author who may post updates on the Bradt website at 📱 bradtguides.com/updates. Alternatively you can add a review of the book to 📱 bradtguides.com or Amazon.

TRAINSCOTTING!

I think most of the world would like to be **SCOTTISH**. All the Americans
who come here never look for English blood or Welsh, only for Scottish
and Irish. It's understandable. The Scots effectively created the face of
the **MODERN** world: the railways, the bridges, the tunnels.
Joanna Lumley

Like the land of Scotland itself, the nation's railways show astonishing contrasts and high points within a fairly small span of the globe. And just how good are these lines? Well, we have been officially informed that this little country offers you the most beautiful scenic railway, not just in Scotland, not just in the UK, not just in Europe, but *in the whole world!*

Scotland is, truth be told, a land of railway superlatives. As well as the MOST SCENIC line in the world, it offers the MOST ROMANTIC rail journeys in Britain. The HIGHEST main-line summits. The LONGEST bridge. The HIGHEST railway viaduct. The LONGEST AND BOLDEST spans. The GREATEST manmade wonder, some would add. The MOST FAMOUS railway bridge in the world. The two GRANDEST British main lines (one end of each, that is). The MOST NORTHERLY station in Britain, and the MOST WESTERLY too. The MOST SUCCESSFUL standard-gauge timetabled steam service. The BEST railway reopenings and electrification projects. The MOST COMPLEX sleeper operations. Some of the FRIENDLIEST staff, and the LOVELIEST – and sometimes downright quirky – station buildings. And for icing on the cake, or rather cream on the cranachan, some UTTERLY CHARMING preserved lines, steam centres and luxury excursion trains, which cruise through this magnificent land.

The aim of this guide – which follows on from the very well-received *Britain From The Rails: A Window Gazer's Guide* – is to make your journeys more enjoyable, or to whet your appetite beforehand, by pointing out great moments to look out for and telling their stories. There are great railway yarns thrown in too – sometimes very odd, deeply amusing, or just compellingly curious, given that I'm also the author of Bradt's equally successful *Eccentric Britain* series of books.

Now sit back, and let your eyes treasure the ride – at times spectacular, idyllic, hauntingly bleak, sublime and inspirational. As that lovely song *The Bonnie Banks o' Loch Lomond* says:

'O ye'll take the high road, and I'll take the low road…'

You know what? We'll take the railroad!

SCOTTISH SUPERB SUPERLATIVES

Let's put some flesh on the bare bones of those sensational claims.

First the **CONTRASTS**. There are busy suburban stations of Glasgow's intensely complicated network – the biggest in Britain, outside London – with inner-city ones with tracks all over the place, plus fast no-nonsense inter-city routes, electrified, business-like. Then there are tiny one-track halts up in the Highlands, seemingly made of a few planks, where the only onlooker is a seal or an eagle. Just two rails gleaming in the gloaming, and then the welcome lights of a train that will whisk you to the glimmering grandeur of Edinburgh or the exciting bright lights of Glasgow. Going the other way, the speed with which the atmosphere changes as you leave the busy commuterland of Glasgow at, say, Helensburgh Upper, and are rapidly into mountains with superb views, is hard to beat. The landscape – dotted with around 260 stations served by 2,300 trains day, recent figures said – is like no other.

The **MOST BEAUTIFUL SCENIC RAILWAY IN THE WORLD**: This was the judgement voted by *Wanderlust* magazine readers. It's a subjective thing, I know, and as with most things, beauty is in the eye of the beholder. Or, if you are in a buffet car, the beerholder. All I can say is I have travelled the famed lines in India, Norway, right across Europe from Istanbul to Lisbon, everywhere in the United Kingdom, many lines in North America, New Zealand and China. This one is on another level (1,350ft at one point!). I think it *does* merit the most exalted title. Please go and make up your own mind and let me know. As I have said elsewhere in this book and others, the Skye Line and the Highland Main Line come pretty darn close as contenders.

The **MOST ROMANTIC RAIL JOURNEYS** in Britain: That you can traverse the above routes, crossing high moors watched by royal stags, skirting beautiful lochs dotted with impossibly picturesque wooded islands, glimpsing the golden light over the sea – all starting from London on comfortable sleeper trains, or from Edinburgh or Glasgow, is romance unfurling on twin gleaming silver ribbons. Or from grey North Sea to blue Atlantic in one lovely ride. From Tweedy lowlands past many a mountain and loch to end up overlooking the swirling cold seas between Scotland and Orkney. That is real rail romance.

The **HIGHEST MAIN-LINE SUMMITS**. Trains as high as aircraft (well, light aircraft, anyway)! Drumochter Summit is 1,484ft (452m) above sea level. The line is no by-way – it's double track. It is the highest main-line summit in Britain. On that same route you also pass over Slochd Summit – at 1,315ft (401m), it's not quite as high as the second highest in the UK, which is at Corrour Summit on the West Highland Line at 1,347ft (410m) above sea level.

A NOTE ON PHOTOGRAPHY

No pictures were taken for this book by trespassing on railway land without permission, a habit of some enthusiasts which is dangerous and illegal. Furthermore, pictures which appear to have been taken by leaning a head out of windows were not and this practice is lethal from time to time.

On the other hand, you are perfectly entitled to and should take above-ground pictures of our wonderful railway heritage and scenery, so long as you do not use a flash, which can blind drivers to important signals. And don't you let any busybody prodnose tell you otherwise.

The LONGEST RAIL BRIDGE. At 2¼ miles (3,264m), the Tay Bridge is the longest in Britain, and the shameful story of its predecessor's collapse and how this led to another superlative – Scotland's worst poem – is on page 69.

The HIGHEST RAILWAY VIADUCT in Britain is Ballochmyle Viaduct, 169ft (52m) over the Water of Ayr between Kilmarnock and Auchinleck in East Ayrshire. Yes the track is even higher than that on the Forth Bridge. Completed in March 1848, and engineer John Miller's masterpiece, the viaduct was then the largest masonry arch in the world, and indeed still looks sensational from below. Glasgow to Carlisle passenger trains and heavy freights still traverse it daily.

The WIDEST AND BOLDEST SPANS. The globally famous Forth Bridge is a stupendous achievement. Two of the spans leap 1,710ft (520m) across at a clearance of 150ft (46m) above high water. So get your tides right and you can get the biggest warships ever built for the Royal Navy out from Rosyth Docks nearby. Which they do. But it is the height and striking lozenge shape of the cantilever construction that makes it so recognisable. And this bridge also lays Scotland's claim to have the GREATEST MANMADE WONDER in Britain and to the MOST FAMOUS RAILWAY BRIDGE in the world. Full story on page 72. Plus, we should mention historically, the WORLD'S FIRST TRAIN FERRY (see box, page 58).

The MOST NORTHERLY RAILWAY STATION is Thurso. A Viking name, and a unique spot, overlooking Britain's most northerly headland and Orkney. Read about it, and the train that tried to get further north, on page 170.

The MOST WESTERLY RAILWAY STATION in Britain is not, as many might imagine, down at the end of Cornwall, but at Arisaig, on the Mallaig extension of the West Highland Line. This staggeringly beautiful route offers great views of the islands of Rum, Eigg and Muck, the start and finish of Britain's shortest river, and the deepest loch too. Arisaig is also unique because of the four cardinal compass points on Britain's railway network, it is the only one that is not a terminus. See page 131.

The **MOST SUCCESSFUL STANDARD-GAUGE TIMETABLED STEAM OPERATION**, the incomparable *Jacobite* train. And with the Glenfinnan Viaduct making global fame through its starring role in the Harry Potter films, when the *Hogwarts Express* traverses the viaduct accompanied by flying Ford Anglia cars – see my comments on page 127 – more people are visiting and finding that this unique place works its spell on them. Indeed, well over 70,000 people have enjoyed the magic of the *Jacobite*. Long may it continue.

The **BEST RAILWAY REOPENINGS AND ELECTRIFICATION PROJECTS**. An Englishman, a Welshman and an Irishman gathered in a pub (and this will be a right let-down if you are expecting the usual joke!) and said: 'You know what, you've got to hand it to the Scots on railway progress.' Whole new lines have been built – such as the Borders Railway (page 107), new electrification has been rolled out between Edinburgh and Glasgow, both main lines to England have long been electrified for 125mph trains, new or reopened branches are opening (such as Alloa, reopened in 2008). Meanwhile the rest of the UK has dithered and dallied – electrification to Swansea stopped short, to the English Midlands from London is stopped at the time of writing, which means even when working under electric power, trains have to lug diesel engines and fuel tanks back and forth. The Welsh Valley Lines were to be all electrified, and then it was put in doubt for a while. It's a shameful shambles, while Scotland shows how it should be done. Clean hydro or wind power running trains making no pollution and little noise. Brilliant!

Not that Scotland should rest on her laurels. Finish the Borders Railway down through Hawick to Carlisle. Reopen those mothballed lines in Fife. Get the Edinburgh Suburban and Southside Junction Railway stations up and running again. Get the Glasgow Airport branch built. Reconnect St Andrews. Crack on, Scotland, and continue to show us how it's done.

The **MOST COMPLEX SLEEPER OPERATIONS**. Two enormously long sleeper trains leave London every night, and two more in the opposite direction. The second one, which goes only to Edinburgh and Glasgow, splits at Carstairs, and leaves so late one can enjoy an evening out in London's West End and then awake refreshed in one of those cities. Marvellous. The first one is the really romantic one, the *Highlander*. It leaves earlier, and splits at Edinburgh into three trains, usually of five carriages going to Fort William, five for Aberdeen (which also serves Dundee) and six for Inverness.

All these portions need their own locos and crews for each leg – and while this is happening, it's going on in the reverse direction too. Britain's only other sleeper service is the simpler *Cornish Riviera* from London Paddington straight to Penzance. To make it really worthwhile, Cornwall needs lengthening by about 200 miles!

And finally, some of the FRIENDLIEST staff and the LOVELIEST – or sometimes downright quirky – station buildings. Well I have to admit I'm biased. You'll have to have a look for yourself. Let me know what you think…

WHO IS THIS BOOK FOR?
A LOT OF PEOPLE

- Visitors to Scotland, and Britain, including those who have bought BritRail passes and want to know how to get the very best out of their tour. Rail tourism is growing in Scotland.
- Green travellers who believe that flying or driving long distances to see beautiful places is also helping to destroy them. The carbon footprint of an electric train powered by hydro, wind or nuclear power, or even the other train braking on its way down the same hill, is zero. While that's the ideal, any train is ten times better than any plane in pollution terms. Some trains are now powered by biodiesel. And Scotland has been brilliant in gathering green power from wind and water (both, you might sometimes agree, in rather good supply!), and applying it in electrification projects far more successfully than England and Wales.
- Home-grown holidaymakers and day trippers who don't know where to start. I was approached by just such a lady at a travel show and she suggested this book's predecessor (page 177).
- People who already travel by train, including commuters, who want to know some fascinating stories about their lines. Heroism, murder, mayhem, blood, beauty, brilliance, humour – it's all between the lines. Local history fans too. Making the tracks you thought you knew a lot more fun.
- 'Romantics', who want to travel in style and really experience the country rather than being jammed in an Economy-Class aircraft and set down in a strange place, with no sense of getting there. To see the landscape for yourself, without looking at the back of a lorry or the road surface in front of you. Nowhere in the world betters Scotland's landscapes on the right day.
- Rail fans who want to hear more fascinating titbits about their favourite routes, the history, the weird accidents and the odd characters, and are open to suggestions for new routes.
- People who don't, won't or can't drive or fly.
- People who love Scotland, with its magnificent landscapes, its heritage of glorious cities with world-class attractions and museums, castles and pubs, charming country towns with wonderful shops, quirky customs and cathedrals (not forgetting viaducts, stations and tunnels) and want to know what to look out for. Incredible journeys, indelible memories!

The only people this book isn't especially aimed at are those who want to list all the locomotive classes by numbers and map every station on the system and their long-gone timetables. I don't have the room, and I want this to be more interesting than any list, fascinating though that may be to that very eccentric British breed, the trainspotter. All I can say to anyone of that persuasion is that you, too, will find stories in here to intrigue, amuse and fascinate, and you don't need me to explain the difference between 4472 and 4468 anyway!

HOW TO USE THIS BOOK

This isn't a mile-by-mile description of every single route. That would require something like the thickest phone book you ever saw, not too great for travelling with. And, frankly, some routes are just not that exciting, only useful for getting from A to B and passing through relatively ordinary places (actually that isn't entirely true – researching this and other books I found that everywhere, however unattractive, has *something* interesting).

While the system is outlined in this book, the maze of suburban Glasgow lines is not detailed. Rather, what you have here are just the best: terrific treasures and genuine gems, with the detailed information you need to fully enjoy these lines from one end to the other, plus background features that will enhance the ride. You may have favourite lines you feel I have overlooked; drop me a line about your line, and I'll do the research for the next edition (✉ info@bradtguides.com).

WHAT THE SYMBOLS MEAN

Asterisks have been used throughout the book to rate certain lines, stations and features in terms of their scenery and interest. They will also be used in the text to alert you to bits you should put down your newspaper for:

      ✳ Well worth a look
     ✳✳ Really interesting and beautiful
    ✳✳✳ Terrific
   ✳✳✳✳ A rare treat
  ✳✳✳✳✳ A simply staggering life-changing cosmic experience (this happens only once)

✋ denotes a **request stop**. Standing on the platform waving will probably get you a hoot from the driver, who will stop. But you have to tell the guard well in advance if you're stopping off at one of these – it's no good saying so as you sail through, and in the Highlands it can be a long walk back.

In the **route descriptions**, each station is listed **like this**, as we pass it. A branch line or connecting route is written **LIKE THIS** when you can take it. Major railway features such as viaducts and junctions are written *like this*. Journey times quoted are for the fastest normal trains.

MAPS

Some very useful maps are published in this book, and on featured routes. Maps are schematic for clarity and show what order stations go in, without any accurate representation of the distances between them or real geography.

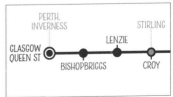

PLANNING YOUR TRIPS
THE BASIC LAYOUT

No railway in Scotland is dull. They are truly one of the best things about this special country, and rail is the best way to enjoy the Highlands, by a long chalk. The 'iron road to the isles' does romance and beauty by the trainload.

But you need to know the layout and plan ahead up there. The basic layout of Scottish railways is like a letter 'H' with the Highland routes being on long unconnected upward arms and the two main lines to England and London being the lower ones, again unconnected (north of the border). The cross bar is the central Lowlands belt between Glasgow on the left (west) and Edinburgh on the right (east).

Of course it's not quite that simple. Both Highland arms have two long branches off them. And once you get near the Lowlands, things get complex with most cities such as Perth and Dundee enjoying separate routes to Glasgow and Edinburgh. These cross at places where you change trains to the other major city. In fact there are five Edinburgh–Glasgow routes.

In the southwest there are also two long secondary routes: one from Glasgow to Ayr and Stranraer (for ferries to Northern Ireland), the other through Dumfries to rejoin the West Coast Main Line at Carlisle. And Inverness is not only reached via the East Coast Main Line but also a wonderful line right up the middle. However, the fact remains that you can't get from one arm of the H to another without going through the central belt.

GLASGOW & EDINBURGH TERMINI

Glasgow Queen Street (for the lines to the Highlands and eastwards to Edinburgh) to **Glasgow Central** (for lines to the southwest and England) is very walkable, even with a medium wheeled suitcase, so I wouldn't bother with the 'Clockwork Orange' underground (subway) which goes only vaguely near each end. There's also a free bus for those holding onward rail tickets, but unless you've got three babies, an infirm granny, huge suitcases, hailstorm overhead or a gammy leg (or all five, in which case my sympathies), why bother?

Central was originally run by the Caledonian Railway and is the terminus of the route from London Euston and others south of the Clyde. Queen Street was the North British outfit and serves routes to the east and north, plus the north bank of the Clyde.

Queen Street is not as lovely as Central (which I enthuse about on page 38). Its layout has always been hampered by the fact that it immediately concentrates all the tracks into a dank, steep tunnel upwards. Originally, this was worked by a cable system because early steam locos couldn't manage it. After that way

GLENFINNAN VIADUCT

AIRBORNE LENS, VISITSCOTLAND

of operating finished, a steam train was once puffing and snorting so hard in the fume-filled tunnel that the driver failed to notice that it was slipping backwards, until it re-emerged humiliatingly in the station he'd just left! Of course back then the tunnel was wreathed in Stygian gloom. Today's diesels have less trouble and a lot less smoke. Vestygian gloom, possibly.

Given that danger of trains running down the hill – now completely under control with severe speed limits, I must add for nervous types – it's odd that the buffer stops are a lot less substantial than those at Central. There probably wasn't room here, as the longest trains just squeeze in sometimes. Safely.

There are also initially unseen low-level lines and platforms at the termini, but these mainly run in suburban networks. The station has now been much improved, with a smart new glass frontage facing George Square.

Edinburgh Waverley is the only open British station named after a novel (now that Westward Ho! station in the West Country has closed). Author Walter Scott's totally over-the-top statue stands nearby. Waverley, in fact a through station not a terminus, is sensationally located in the deep trough between the Old Town and castle on one side and Princes Street and the New Town on the other. Once this was a defensive lake, the Norloch, but the draining of that left a deep cleft in which a massive railway and its station could be located without damaging the wonderful heritage and superb cityscape all around. It's a gem, and Edinburgh has **Haymarket** as another

USEFUL NUMBERS

Caledonian MacBrayne (ferries to the islands) ☎ 0800 066 5000 🖱 calmac.co.uk
Culloden Moor Monument Bus No 5 from Inverness (six miles) ☎ 0844 493 2159
Glenfinnan Monument ☎ 0844 493 2221
Rapsons Buses Skye, Fort William, Inverness ☎ 0871 200 2233
Royal Highland Hotel Inverness (next to station, recommended) ☎ 01463 231926

major station in the West End. Add in the fact that Scotland believes in railways, with Edinburgh having two new (or reopened) routes and Glasgow having expansion too, and the picture is pretty positive north of the border. My favourite small terminus is **Inverness**.

PLANNING AHEAD IN SCOTLAND

Plan ahead and check timetables in Scotland. It could save you time, as in the Highlands the trains are few and the lines are long. For instance, I sauntered down to Inverness station for the 09.35 train and sought a connection to Oban via Glasgow Queen Street. Result: a 12-hour journey (which didn't matter as I had much to do in Glasgow). Had I caught the 07.55 train, however, it would have taken just seven hours 48 minutes. By the way, this illustrates what I was saying on page xv about how you can't get from one arm of the H shape of Scotland's railways to another without going to the central belt.

Highland travel is in proper mountains, and even modern trains are not immune from the temperature changes. Carry a jumper and raincoat even in summer; in winter it is just possible snow will stop the train, so don't turn up in Jimmy Choo heels and a flimsy dress (and that applies to women, too).

First Class is very good and comfortable, but don't assume this is available on all the Highland lines: most branches are Standard Class only. Check when booking. All the long-distance services have trolley catering, and some a counter service. Even short lines such as the Oban branch usually have catering. Not Lowland commuter and city branches, naturally.

If the fewer trains on the remoter lines require planning ahead (rather than just turning up at the station), journeys involving ferries and islands need even more careful planning. But they are wonderful and absolutely worth it.

SEND US YOUR SNAPS!

We'd love to follow your adventures using our *Scotland from the Rails* guide – why not tag us in your photos and stories on Twitter (🐦 @BradtGuides) and Instagram (📷 @bradtguides)?

POSTERS FROM THE PAST

servation Coach Train at Lochy Viaduct near Fort William

THE WEST HIGHLAND LINE

BRITISH RAILWAYS **SEE BRITAIN BY TRAIN**

You tak' the high road and I'll tak' the rail road

and I'll be in Scotland 'afore ye

ASK AT STATIONS & AGENCIES FOR DETAILS OF THE MANY

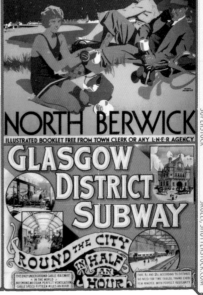

NORTH BERWICK
ILLUSTRATED BOOKLET FREE FROM TOWN CLERK OR ANY L·N·E·R AGENCY

GLASGOW DISTRICT SUBWAY

ROUND THE CITY IN HALF AN HOUR

THE ONLY UNDERGROUND CABLE RAILWAY IN THE WORLD
NO SMOKE NO DIRT PERFECT VENTILATION
CABLE SPEED FIFTEEN MILES AN HOUR

FARE 1d AND 2d ACCORDING TO DISTANCE

The sun always shone and life seemed much simpler if you believe the image sold by charming old railway posters.

1

THE
IRON MEN
AND THEIR
IRON ROAD

FROM BRILLIANT PIONEERS TO THRILLING TRAINS

Scotland's railways go back way further than most people would possibly imagine, and from their Victorian glory days onwards have included more drama and danger, more stupendous feats, more technical leaps forward than most human achievements. Mud, blood, steam, speed, glamour, safety and luxury are all in the story – here's a few snippets from that sensational history.

WAGGONS ROLL!
SCOTLAND'S OLDEST RAILWAY

The scenically sensational line from Inverness to Edinburgh curves round the site of the bloody Battle of Culloden (where Bonnie Prince Charlie's dreams were smashed along with his Jacobite army on 16 April 1746) before soaring high on the beautiful Culloden Viaduct. We have seen elsewhere in the world how railway lines have had to slice through old battlefields.

But, astonishingly, another battle earlier in the Jacobite uprising – the Battle of Prestonpans, a victory for the Highland rebels – was fought on 21 September 1745 *over* a railway line. Not a future one to be laid by the Victorians, but one already there – way before one thinks of railways commonly existing.

Truth be told, it wasn't a railway in the modern sense, but a pioneering evolutionary stage called a waggonway. This, in my book anyway, is Scotland's oldest railway of any sort.

The Tranent to Cockenzie Waggonway in East Lothian was built on wooden rails to haul coal to seaside salt works – salt production was the country's biggest industry at the time. The name of the adjoining fishing town, and the battle, Prestonpans refers to 'priests' pans' where salt was made from seawater. This proto-railway opened in 1722 – that's right, three centuries ago.

The line brought coal north to the coast using horses and gravity, and just horsepower for the empties going back. In more recent years it was used simply as a footpath, with no greater significance known to most people.

But excavations in 2019 revealed the wooden rails and a cobbled horse path between them, about 3ft down.

Ironically, given its role in the 1745 battle, the waggonway's origins were connected to an earlier Jacobite rebellion. The line was built on land seized from followers of the Old Pretender, Bonnie Prince Charlie's father James Edward Stuart, after the failed uprising of 1715. So it was perhaps oddly fitting that about 30 years later the army of his son, the Young Pretender, led Jacobite forces to victory over government troops of King George II at the Battle of Prestonpans, right along the same waggonway. Today the landmark has been marked with a 'Red Wheel' plaque by the Transport Trust.

The 1722 Waggonway Heritage Group has a museum in Cockenzie, so this short but historic railway – its route again rather ironically chopped in half by the 125mph electrified East Coast Main Line, joining with steel bands the two capitals the Jacobites were hoping to wrench apart – is not totally forgotten once again.

As chairman of the group Ed Bethune summed up: 'The Tranent to Cockenzie Waggonway is the birthplace of railways in Scotland. It allowed the potential of the local salt industry to be maximised and subsequently many more lines sprang up throughout Scotland as the benefits of rail for the transport of coal became evident. That this railway was built a full 33 years prior to the Jacobite campaign of 1745 is staggering, and underlines its status as a heritage asset of national importance.' For more details on the route, see 1722waggonway.co.uk.

Note on spelling: The local group uses the old spelling 'waggon', not 'wagon', so we have gone along with that here. You could say they started it all off with a gee-gee!

AN 18TH-CENTURY WAGGON

ARRAN JOHNSTON, WIKIMEDIA COMMONS

THE FIRST 'PROPER' LINES OPEN

It wasn't until a century later that lines we would more easily recognise as railways would start to open. The first regularly used passenger railway was the **KILMARNOCK AND TROON RAILWAY**. It had opened in 1812 as a plateway – that is, running potentially road-going smooth-wheeled waggons on L-shaped rails.

Although this in the long term proved to be a technological dead end in an era of rapid change, it was initially a success and soon took to carrying passengers. However, the design meant that waggon wheels screeched and climbed off the rails – with fatal results for passengers on at least one occasion – and the flat part of the L-shape filled with stones and dirt, causing slow speeds, bumpy rides, friction and breakages. It was later converted to a normal railway with flanges on the train wheels rather than the rails. (This smooth running along the top of the rail is in fact what makes trains so efficient, quiet, fast and comfortable, by the way. Because the wheels are slightly cone-shaped, they steer themselves and the flanges should not come into contact with the rails when smooth running on plain track.)

The partly realigned route still runs for freight and passengers between Kilmarnock and Barassie – the junction for Troon. As was often the case with early purely local lines, the original gauge – the gap between the rails – was 4ft, because no-one envisaged a connected network, so it had to be converted to the 4ft 8½in standard gauge later when it became obvious connection to a network would be needed.

Then in 1826 the **MONKLAND AND KIRKINTILLOCH RAILWAY** opened to feed coal into the Forth and Clyde Canal, and, because it used proper lines and flanged wheels, is considered by some the first proper railway in Scotland. It was very successful, and public in the sense that other freight operators could use it: many of Scotland's early railways were like toll roads, meaning anyone could use them for a fee. However, the M&KR's short malleable iron 'fish-belly' rails (see page 4 for a sketch), good enough for horse-drawn waggons, hindered the introduction of locomotives, needed as connections and branches grew – which further meant it had to be converted from the 'wrong' gauge of 4ft 6in. The earliest use of a passenger coach on this line was in 1828, and it connected the canal boats in a through service – another first.

By the 1850s the main Scottish cities were becoming busily connected, and lines built across the border to England too. By 1900 most towns in Scotland, large or small, had their railway in an intricate network. Yet after World War I, road and air competition began to eat into any profits – and the tide of history began to ebb. Closures began, although these gathered pace considerably after World War II when those lost profits became severe losses.

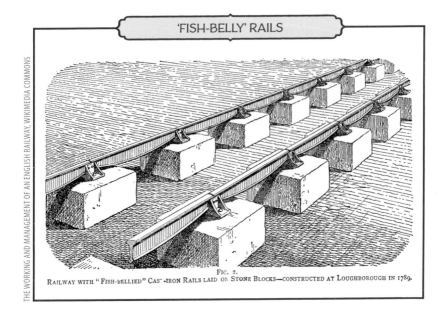

'FISH-BELLY' RAILS

Fic. 2.
RAILWAY WITH "FISH-BELLIED" CAST-IRON RAILS LAID ON STONE BLOCKS—CONSTRUCTED AT LOUGHBOROUGH IN 1789.

Oddly enough, by modern thinking, when the system was rationalised in 1923 into 'the big four' there wasn't much impetus to have a purely *Scottish* railway. Scots argued against it, saying they would rather have competition between the Euston-based London Midland and Scottish Railway and the London and North Eastern Railway, based at King's Cross, because both those big groups had the money, equipment and expertise to run things well. In fact, even earlier than that the term 'North British' was used for one major railway company, an identity that had come into vogue after Scotland's 18th-century setbacks; strangely by modern thinking, some Scots wanted to be considered 'North Britons'. I do recall the great North British Hotel in Princes Street, Edinburgh (now the Balmoral, still wonderful).

A few decades on, and Scotland was becoming very much its own country again, more confident in its unique identity, going from strength to strength, regaining at the very end of the century a Scottish Parliament which had been abandoned on union with England in 1701. This political process is reflected in the railways – in 1948 when nationalised British Railways was created, Scotland got its own region. In recent times, the trains were called ScotRail, with a stylised saltire on their sides.

But through all these changes, Scotland's fabulous pioneering railways have strived, served and mostly – sometimes against the odds – survived. Thank goodness, we should think as we climb aboard for another unforgettable railway trip!

THRILLS & SPILLS IN A DRAMATIC CENTURY

The 100 years from 1850 to 1950 saw Scotland's railways go through sensational, exciting phases one after the other. None of these things could have been imagined at the start, and the dangers and gains were both immense – and the cost in lives, too. But the progress and bold innovation has been simply phenomenal. Here, in a limited-stop express run, are six giant leaps forward that will be more fully dealt with in the relevant chapters:

THE TAY BRIDGE (1879)

Scotland's and Britain's longest railway bridge, 2¼ miles, connecting Fife and Edinburgh north across the Firth of Tay to Dundee, this bridge also attracted other less favourable superlatives: the worst disaster, when the first bridge fell down taking a passenger train with it on 28 December 1879; the worst poem about a disaster ever written, the one by the awful William McGonagall; and the biggest fall from grace of a previously much-praised engineer, Sir Thomas Bouch. But today it's a lovely ride on a much stronger totally storm-proof bridge. More on page 69.

THE FLOATING RAILWAY (1850)

This is a fascinating but totally forgotten side-story. What did the railway companies do before the Forth Bridge was built? The answer is that an engineering genius – later depicted as a bit of a villain – created a whole new concept: the 'floating railway'. Thomas Bouch, known for his engineering work on the Tay Bridge, designed and built the first link span, the tilting ramp that allows all today's ferries to roll traffic, road or rail, on and off a ship at differing states of tide. The first train ferry on the Forth (and in the world), using the specially built *Leviathan*, began service on 3 February 1850, was a huge success and was to change ferry technology for ever. See page 58 for more.

THE FORTH BRIDGE (1890)

You must have heard of the Forth Bridge and know its iconic three-lozenge-shaped outline. The most famous railway bridge in the world, it joins Edinburgh northwards to Fife and gives further access to Dundee and Aberdeen. It has starred in numerous films and books, is 1½ miles long, has towers 360ft tall and contains 55,000 tons of steel and 8 million rivets. Thrilling to ride across, intriguing to read about, and well worth a walk around at either end. Details on page 58.

'THE RACE TO THE NORTH' (1880S & '90S)

Involving derring-do and dastardly deeds, this was about the bitter rivalry between the two groups of companies that operated what are now called the West Coast and East Coast Main Lines to Scotland. Safe speed limits were dangerously exceeded as trains hurtled round curves at break-neck speeds. It's amazing that there wasn't a huge crash. Read more on page 78.

THE WEST HIGHLAND LINE (1894)

This book makes no apology for getting excited by the world's most scenic railway line, but what stupendous efforts were needed to get the iron road to the isles up into those mountains and across bleak, boggy Rannoch Moor! And what dramatic innovations, quirky anecdotes and above all sheer beauty were and are involved. See page 115 for the story of this wonderful line, and its piano-playing branch to Oban (it's a very strange safety device!). And then, of course, there are the almost-as-good Highland Main Line (page 135), Skye Line (page 151) and Far North Line (page 163) to savour and remember as well.

QUINTINSHILL (1915)

In the box on page 88, we tell the tragic tale of Scotland's worst railway disaster. But the Quintinshill disaster and its aftermath, macabre though it was, in fact proves directly how much safer railways have become, step by step. We can be quite certain such a thing can never happen again. A terrible tragedy, but it also led to a giant leap forward in terms of safety. And does reading about *Titanic* make one nervous catching a ferry across from Oban to Mull? Of course not!

GOING LOCO ON WORLD RECORDS

Because Scotland enjoys the north end of each of Britain's two premier rail routes – the East Coast Main Line from Edinburgh to London and the West Coast Main Line from Glasgow to London – this has meant it has seen the most thrilling railway developments over more than a century. For instance, take the late 19th-century 'Stirling Singles', created by Kilmarnock-born engineer Patrick Stirling, which sped over the ECML. They were so-called because they had one huge 8ft 1in driving wheel each side, making them look a bit like a land-going paddle-steamer, but given to very fast running. They took part in the aforementioned 'Race to the North' in 1895. More often seen in Scotland were the same engineer's previous design for the

Glasgow and South-Western Railway, on which Stirling Singles were based. Brilliant engines for their era!

Then you have the most famous locomotives of all time racing up and down to Scotland in the period between the two world wars. History tends – rightly – to focus on the acclaimed trail-blazers such as *Flying Scotsman* – the first authenticated loco to run at 100mph in 1934 and the first non-stop Edinburgh–London run (full, fascinating story on page 24) – or *Mallard*, designed by the same Scottish genius, Sir Nigel Gresley, which grabbed the world steam record in 1938 at 126mph (and will probably never relinquish it; more on page 16). But one shouldn't overlook in that glorious, glamorous era the streamlined luxury named trains (as opposed to just locomotives) such as the beautifully turned-out *Silver Jubilee* on the ECML or the *Coronation Scot* on the WCML. These trains featured previously unimagined luxuries, with plush dining cars, smoking saloons with armchairs and sofas, hairdressers, a cinema, secretaries and typing pools – you name it.

The latter were sometimes pulled by the powerful Coronation class locos often named after a Duchess: some were elegantly streamlined (the curvy ones) and some not (square-enders). You can imagine, by the way, the schoolboy laughter not so long ago when newspapers were offered a picture with the subject field (if I recall rightly) 'A curvy Duchess blowing off at Watford Junction'. Particularly as most newspaper staff nowadays would have

A 'STIRLING SINGLE'

no idea what they were talking about. It was the safety valves roaring on *Duchess of Sutherland,* Platform 8, if I remember! I am not sure that she wore the 'curvy' air-smoothed casing at that time, so may be misremembering that detail. She was always a bit frisky, that Duchess. (And if you don't like that sense of humour, please don't Google 'Stirling Singles' – not unless you are a lonely heart in that Scottish city!)

Post-World War II the line to Edinburgh saw advance after advance, with the hugely powerful diesel locos, the Deltics, which being two-stroke diesels smoked, howled and moaned their way up and down the East Coast Main Line like low-flying V-bombers. The engines were of a brilliant secret design for wartime motor torpedo boats. A reader comment on one of my earlier books said the name 'Deltic' was short for diesel electric (where the drive to the wheels is electric); actually no, Sir, all diesel locos are like that (bar a few shunters, etc). What made these unique, and gave them their name, was the engine layout like the Greek letter delta – a triangle in cross section. Three crankshafts in the formation with the cylinders facing towards each other, or rather the pistons sharing cylinders from either end. Brilliant but noisy. If you get to see one in action – or on film – you'll see what I mean. The fact that there were very few of these striking Class 55 engines – 22 I think – and they had evocative names of famous regiments (such as *The Fife and Forfar Yeomanry*) or racehorses (*Nimbus, Pinza*) made them eminently recognisable even to those who were not trainspotters. Mind you, people could think they were steam trains coming if the engines were emitting towers of smoke. They were that polluting!

Later still came the brilliantly successful High-Speed Train (or Class 43, marketed as InterCity 125), nicknamed the 'Flying Bananas' because of their pointed yellow ends, which could do 140mph, and gained the world diesel record. Following in the tracks of the famed A4 steam locos such as *Mallard*, these have now also retired from the ECML to do sterling work – even Stirling work! – between Scottish cities today. Oddly enough, these trains were created as a stop-gap when another design failed, but arguably they were Britain's most comfortable and successful train ever. Do people like them? One fan said as the first one arrived north of the border: 'Hail the new king of Scotland!'

And then there was electrification, a set of increasingly reliable 140mph-capable pollution-free trains ending with the latest *Azuma* class, built in Britain by Japanese 'bullet train' company Hitachi (Azuma sounds like a name made up by a marketing twerp, but is an archaic Japanese word meaning 'east', appropriately). I say ending with, but the story will surely go on. This capital-to-capital route is always the grandest line in Britain and by far the best way to arrive in Scotland to start a rail tour (more on page 11). So book up now, and take your window seat for a richly rewarding railway experience.

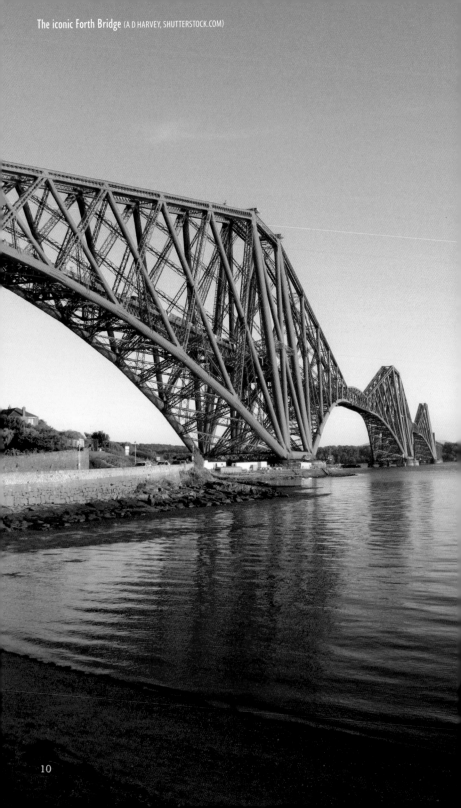

The iconic Forth Bridge (A D HARVEY, SHUTTERSTOCK.COM)

GREAT ARRIVALS

The Famed Main Lines

A pologies if it seems strange that a book about Scotland contains a section about England, but as we heartily recommend arriving in Scotland by the East Coast Main Line, bear with us. (The West Coast Main Line has its high points too – literally at Shap – but I've covered only part of the route as the English section does not warrant a mile-by-mile description.) For resident Scots, regard this as a bonus chapter, and when returning home, we are confident you'll find points of interest. And you should not, in our view, chop a glorious railway like the East Coast Main Line, from London to Edinburgh to Dundee and Aberdeen, into lesser pieces! To put it another way, you wouldn't have an account of the Orient Express that just did the Austrian parts, would you?

GETTING TO EDINBURGH***
THE EAST COAST MAIN LINE
4½HRS TO EDINBURGH, 393 MILES

Lots of main lines reckon they are important, but the East Coast Main Line really is the business. It has speed, style and scenery in abundance, and shoots north from London like an arrow across flatlands to reach the Scottish capital with no diversions. It has always had romance, records, racecourse speeds, relative reliability and real respect as a senior railway compared with the tiddler tramways – as fans of this line would see it – down south. It doesn't look down its nose at lesser railways, however, in the way that the Great Western always has. It doesn't need to. It's the no-nonsense chieftain of British railways, starting in the business-like terminus at King's Cross, arriving in the heart of Edinburgh and reaching right up to Aberdeen and yet, oddly, going through only one really big city – Newcastle – en route. The ECML, as it is known, features iconic landmarks, fascinating history and stunning scenery that are rare in such a modern high-speed main line. All aboard!

NEWCASTLE,
EDINBURGH
YORK
MIDLANDS········ SCARBOROUGH
LEEDS ······································HULL
DONCASTER
SHEFFIELD·············· LINCOLN
NEWARK·
NORTHGATE
·SKEGNESS
NOTTINGHAM·······●·GRANTHAM
LEICESTER········· LINCOLN
PETERBOROUGH◎
ELY, NORWICH
HUNTINGDON
HITCHIN· CAMBRIDGE,
ELY, NORWICH
STEVENAGE· HERTFORD
KNEBWORTH
WELWYN NORTH·
WELWYN
GARDEN CITY
HATFIELD·
POTTERS BAR
ALEXANDRA
PALACE
HERTFORD
HARRINGAY
HORNSEY·
LUTON AIRPORT, FINSBURY PARK
EAST MIDLANDS EUROSTAR
(ST PANCRAS) TO PARIS,
BRUSSELS
(ST PANCRAS)
LONDON
KING'S CROSS
WEST MIDLANDS,
SCOTLAND VIA WCML
(EUSTON)

KING'S CROSS TO YORK*
RECORD BREAKERS
2HRS, 188 MILES

What a brilliant reconstruction of King's Cross was completed in 2014. Look at the way the ingenious and magnificent roof arches across what was wasted space between the terminus and the old Great Northern Hotel – it's like being inside a giant fountain! It replaces the shabby cabins that messed up the frontage for decades and caused overcrowding. Well done, Network Rail, Camden Council and architect John McAslan. And what a wonderful contrast the simple, ascetic 1852 building designed by Lewis Cubitt makes with the Gothic madness of St Pancras next door, also brilliantly restored.

If you're a Harry Potter fan – and half the world is – then first pop across to under the footbridge in the departure concourse near to the suburban platforms to not see Platform 9¾, or at least see its sign, where potty Potter people pose with a trolley halfway through the wall. The platform itself is invisible, but you would want the *Hogwarts Express* to Hogsmeade if you do get through the wall. If you're not a fan, you'll think I'm bonkers, so don't bother. King's Cross station also appears in dozens of books and films ranging from *The Ladykillers* to Sherlock Holmes, and is on the site of Queen Boadicea's grave, says the legend.

IF YOU HAVE THE CHOICE, SIT ON THE RIGHT-HAND SIDE OF YOUR TRAIN, FACING FORWARD.

The start of what is generally a remarkably level route to Edinburgh could not be more up and down. The converging tracks from the various platforms – known as the throat – dive into *Gasworks Tunnel* under the Regent's Canal, which, having been built around 1820, got there first. Being wet, it wasn't easily made into a humpback bridge, so the railway had to dive under (or, at the St Pancras terminus next door, over). A lot of bother for something hardly used. Climbing again after the dip – which used to give long steam-hauled trains such a jerk that they could be in danger of breaking their couplings – we pass under a new large grey-tube bridge which carries the Eurostars from Paris and Brussels heading for adjacent St Pancras at 186mph. Well, not at that point, clearly, as it would be *zut alors* and

REMINDER‼ **✳ = SCENIC RATING**

ooh la la! as they pranged into the buffers, but they do that speed between here and the Chunnel. Oddly, at this point, trains heading for Paris are aimed roughly towards Oslo.

Even higher still is a bridge carrying the North London Line east–west, and deep beneath us somewhere nearby are many Underground lines, including a disused narrow-gauge Post Office one, and tunnels linking surface lines to Tube lines, making this the spaghetti junction of railways and canals. And King's Cross is just one of five huge termini almost in a row between here and Paddington. Parliament insisted they go no further south.

Climbing up again into the daylight, the massive Emirates Stadium of Arsenal Football Club is soon on the right, with the remains of its Art Deco predecessor visible further away as we speed through **Finsbury Park**.

After whizzing through **Hornsey** and **Harringay**, the massive site on a hill on the left is Alexandra Palace, or 'Ally Pally' as Londoners fondly know it. It's the twin of Crystal Palace on the similar hill on the opposite, south rim of the Thames Basin: they both had huge halls of popular entertainment (the Crystal Palace being burnt down in the 1930s), both had television transmitter towers, and both had their own branch lines, both now gone.

After **Alexandra Palace** station a line takes off on our left and goes up and over to the right. This is the start of the **HERTFORD LOOP** which rejoins our East Coast Main Line around 20 miles later, a pattern of connections which recurs many times down this route. It is a useful diversionary route if anything blocks the narrow section at Welwyn ahead, and indeed if you're taking it while the main line is closed for repairs, a pleasant if not over-fast ramble through leafy northern suburbs into Hertfordshire, and only a mile or so longer.

Here on the main line, however, the route tunnels repeatedly through the low hills. As we pass **Potters Bar**, the gin-'n'-Jag belt of wealthy golf-playing commuters surrounds us. **Hatfield**, after some curves, is

MARY EVANS PICTURE LIBRARY

the site of the erstwhile De Havilland aircraft factory, home of the 'wooden wonder' Mosquito of World War II, the Comet and the 146 Whisper-jet.

Welwyn Garden City, next, was set up by idealist Ebenezer Howard, who thought workers could live in leafy suburbs instead of slums, away from factories, which should be confined to industrial areas. Actually it was his second attempt, the first being near Hitchin further up this line, at Letchworth Garden City. Because the rest of the world copied them, they are rather boring nowadays (a bit like Aldous Huxley going on about zip fasteners as a fantastic futuristic thing in his book *Brave New World*). But garden cities changed the world: every neat suburb is descended from them.

Watch out just north of here, just after the tracks narrow (from four to two), for the superb *Digswell Viaduct**, built with 13 million bricks, on which we soar above the leafy garden city in style. The train then rockets through **Welwyn North** and two tunnels, and regains four tracks beyond the bottleneck (which may be widened during the lifetime of this book) caused by these landmarks. **Knebworth**, of rock festival fame, follows.

Just before **Stevenage**, the HERTFORD LOOP rejoins from our right in a burrowing junction (that is, not a flying junction, as when it left us at Ally Pally – see page 13). Stevenage is recognisable at speed from the brick towers on the platforms, and within a few miles we are into **Hitchin**, 32 miles from King's Cross, where a flat junction has for many decades let the CAMBRIDGE LINE curve off to our right, next stop Letchworth Garden City. That's all three types of junction in one paragraph.

Flat junctions, however, are a flaming nuisance, as twice an hour a Cambridge-bound train had to cross all three other tracks of the ECML, bringing Britain's premier railway to a grinding halt.

So hey presto! – a brand-new flyover a mile or so north of Hitchin lets Cambridge-bound trains take off east without blocking the others. It's just one of dozens of investments in the past decade which are making the system work much better – improvements which would have been a pipe dream in the dreadful, depressing decades of shrinking the railways from 1963 to 2003.

The river at the small market town of Hitchin is the Hiz (in droughts, should it be the Hizn't?) and we have now left the Thames Basin. Whereas the rivers further south – such as the charmingly named Mimram, which flows under the Digswell Viaduct – flow into the Thames, from here on they come out in The Wash (as your granny may have said most things do), which is that huge square inlet of the North Sea above East Anglia.

As we speed through Ickleford village – where the ancient Icknield Way fords the river – and into Bedfordshire, the countryside becomes more open, wet, fertile, flat and ideal for high-speed railways. The first village, **Arlesey**, once had a huge mental hospital called Arlesey Asylum – unfortunately the source of more than a few suicides on the line. It was renamed Three Counties Hospital and then Fairfield in that odd way of renaming things to make them seem more pleasant.

Now, relax. There's nothing much to see except productive farmland and glimpses of the almost-parallel A1 road to Edinburgh – sometimes still known by its old name, the Great North Road – as we speed through small towns and see more and more waterways in this increasingly flat fenland. The drainage channels are always wet here, even after much dry weather. Larger towns like **Huntingdon** have stops, but many small villages, such as the eccentrically named Offord D'Arcy and Offord Cluny, just before Huntingdon, pass in a flash with no stations or signs.

Approaching **Peterborough**, the ELY LINE from Cambridge and Norwich joins from the right, passing under us just before the river. When you consider that line needed Whittlesey Mere (the largest lake in southern England) to be drained in 1851 to be built, you can see how wet this area was until recently. The ending '-ey' in Whittlesey meant 'island', as once true at Chelsea, Bermondsey and Battersea in London.

Peterborough appears with its squat cathedral tower on the right and, further down, a mosque. It's a meeting of cultures in other ways too – broad Norfolk voices will be joining the train saying stuff such as 'They didn't say change at Ely, what arr they loike?' contrasting with the sing-song Geordie of the Newcastle train crew and the beautifully clear Edinburgh diction of those heading that far north.

A line south of the station and going west, by the way, links to a rather good steam line, the **NENE VALLEY RAILWAY**, although there are not regular through trains at the time of writing. To get to Peterborough (Nene Valley) station you'd need a bus, car or taxi, although it is walkable for most people. Its main claim to fame is that European-sized trains (bigger in cross section, but same tracks) can fit here, so it's great for making movies supposedly set in Europe. Usually I'm impatient with steam lines that fail to link up with the system, but with the amazingly busy ECML I see it would be difficult here.

Leaving Peterborough, there are *New England freight yards* on the right, with heavy locos standing waiting for their turn. Snowploughs in mid-summer will have an even longer wait, maybe for years this far south.

As we head north, the line that runs parallel on the left for a few miles and then diverges is the **LEICESTER LINE** that goes to Melton Mowbray – and if that makes you think of wagons of pork pies, it's worth noting we have just passed the village of Stilton, as in the cheese. A gourmet express possibly, but then this very route saw Britain's first railway dining car, which left Leeds for London King's Cross on 1 November 1879. The Pullman car *Princess of Wales* carried only ten First Class passengers and the carriage included a gentlemen's smoking room and a ladies' dressing room. Your buffet car today, its direct descendant, is available without paying the two shillings and sixpence (12½p) surcharge. As far as I can see this pretty and useful cross-country connector has no official name or nickname – please put me right if there is one – so we can therefore dub it the Pork Pie line.

Yet another route, the **LINCOLN LINE**, diverges right (east) for Spalding and that fine cathedral city (54 miles). A burrowing junction has just been built here.

Further up here we start climbing Stoke Bank. It is a long, gentle and straight slope, ideal for racing downhill towards London, and as such became the site of a historic moment on 3 July 1938. In conditions of severe secrecy – in case the rival West Coast company LMS tried to steal a march by grabbing the place in the record books – driver Joseph Duddington, a man known to take calculated risks, crested Stoke Summit at the north of the bank at a creditable 75mph, coming towards London. He was driving the LNER's streamlined *Mallard*, a name engraved on the hearts of railwaymen around the world.

The A4-class loco was pulling a carriage with special measuring equipment – a dynamometer car – and although the track was officially passed for only 90mph, he was encouraged to give the Gresley-designed loco her head down the gentle slope. The speed crept up and up and eventually reached 126mph, a world steam record which surely will never be broken.

Now 4468 *Mallard* is exhibited in pride of place at the National Railway Museum, further along this route at York, with plaques on either side proudly stating her world record-holder status.

Other restored examples of this brilliant design still pull trains around the country. But here's a thought: this amazing speed – which severely overheated the mechanical parts so she had to be towed for repair and had the press celebrating the driver as a hero – is matched every day on routes from London by regular trains such as the one you are sitting in.

At the top of Stoke Bank, after passing the 100 miles from London mark, we go through a tunnel and then whistle through **Grantham**. Not whistling madly, one hopes, as the *Scotch Express* was as she hurtled through Grantham against red signals in 1906. She was supposed to stop, but didn't, hitting points set for the severely curved Nottingham route and was wrecked against a bridge parapet. Recent re-examination of the mysterious crash shows that the carriage brakes must have been fixed off by railwaymen zealous not to cause delay at an earlier stop, and not restored, so the driver had only the engine's brake to stop on a slippery rail that night. Thankfully, such an error is now impossible.

Grantham's most famous export was 1980s prime minister Margaret Thatcher. Like the *Mallard* above, she was heading south, tough, novel, unstoppable, and a record-holder – the first woman prime minister, and three-times elected too. But, unlike the *Mallard*, Thatcher had little use for Britain's coal miners.

Talking of coal miners, we are approaching the Trent Valley, where Old King Coal played a massive part in our Industrial Revolution. More on that in a minute though. A line diverges left at Grantham for Nottingham, and after another short tunnel we cross over the route it connects with, the **POACHER LINE** which runs west–east from the city famous for its dastardly Sheriff to Skegness on the North Sea. Skegness was famously promoted with the slogan 'Skegness is so bracing' and the Jolly Fisherman.

The odd thing about the East Coast Main Line is that it misses all the major cities only 20 or so miles to our left (west), such as Leicester, Nottingham, Sheffield, Derby and many more (served by their own Midland Main Line from St Pancras). It thus avoids their associated hills and rivers, racing instead across much flatter country for the prize of York, and later Edinburgh. At **Newark Northgate** we cross the **NOTTINGHAM–LINCOLN LINE** on an unusual and juddering flat crossing. Not unusual for a tram in some eastern European backstreet, but teeth-rattlingly odd for a main line aiming for 125mph speeds. Maybe it'll be replaced with a flyover by the time you get there, but meanwhile let's hope the signalmen keep this rather unnerving junction clear of crossing trains (don't worry, they always do and the safeguards are foolproof). It is often quoted as the only one in Britain. It isn't – there's another at Porthmadog, North Wales, although being mixed gauge, that really *is* unique.

Next we whizz over a recently replaced bridge over a canal – a waterway that still carries much freight, by the way, unlike that annoyingly empty one back at King's Cross – and then over the River Trent. The A1 road to Edinburgh, which has been shadowing us all the way, reappears on our right.

We see power station cooling towers – those massive cylinders taller than cathedral spires, with concave sides – all the way up the Trent Valley, and at one time you can see three sets at once. They are here because the power demand is here, the coal is here (or was), and the river provided transport and cooling water. In fact the railway provided much of the transport, with lines frequently curving off to either power stations or collieries. Of course, no-one had thought of global warming when these things were set up. Ideally, this train would be powered by some windmill or waterfalls up

MUCH-RECOMMENDED SIDE TRIPS FROM YORK

On great lines: Scarborough, on the east coast (42 miles), and inland: interesting Knaresborough (16 miles) and pretty Harrogate (20 miles). By steam train, occasionally.

in the hills. In fact it might be one of these power stations doing the hard work for a few years yet. Odd, when you think about it, that, if so, our sleek electric train is still powered by coal and steam, just as *Mallard* was. Or, possibly, by biomass – wood chips.

We pass an old freight connection at **Dukeries Junction** (the area being so-called because of the enormously powerful landowners including a whole bunch of dukes who lived here and got wealthy on the coal in the 19th century) and then speed through **Retford**, with the low-level station on a line crossing ours visible on the right.

There is more and more evidence of the industrial past as we approach **Doncaster**, Donny to some, a major junction and famous railway works. Lines come in from Lincoln and Derby and, beyond the station, diverge right (east) for Hull on the North Sea and left for Leeds and other Yorkshire towns. We head on towards York, freight lines all over the place, power stations on both sides and loops for coal trains alongside the main line.

One of the places on this route is called Heck, ironically as it turned out. A sleepy driver of a Land Rover pulling a trailer on a road crossing over the railway managed to drive down the embankment and on to the southbound track in 2001. A GNER (the then operating firm, and a good one) InterCity 225 train heading for King's Cross hit it and propelled the wreckage down the track at around 90mph. The leading vehicle, a driving trailer, stayed upright until it struck some points and was diverted by dreadful luck into the path of a freight train heading north. The collision was at an estimated 142mph closing speed, and ten people were killed.

The car driver was jailed for five years, and the young driver of the Freightliner freight train heading north, Steve Dunn, was commemorated with a new locomotive named after him.

In a little-known and bizarre twist, the loco at the back of the GNER train, which was propelling it southwards, had also been involved in a fatal crash at Hatfield a few months earlier (which was due to poor rail maintenance, now totally fixed). GNER renumbered the loco, which was undamaged in both crashes, in case people thought it was jinxed. It was just a coincidence. In 2021, this loco was finally scrapped without any more mishaps.

Perhaps you don't want to read about crashes while you're on a train, but the reason they are interesting is because they are so very rare. Most years go by with no passengers killed on British railways, yet every year sees at least 1,500 road users killed. You could hardly be safer.

They are also interesting in the way the railway industry works: they rarely happen again, because it corrects itself. Road overbridges have been massively strengthened since the Heck crash and longer, stronger crash barriers put up; hundreds of miles of track have been replaced since the Hatfield crash because of a particular problem, and the whole system scrutinised on a far more frequent basis. Whereas on roads, exactly the same stupid crashes happen week after week.

Cheer up, we're approaching **York**** which, when the railway was built was the first town of any real importance on its route north, at around 188 miles out of King's Cross. It is still the most attractive city so far. Things to look out for (and visit if you are stopping): York Minster, the cathedral, on the right; on the left the wonderful National Railway Museum, a branch of the Science Museum worth a whole day out (and free to enter), even if you think trains have steering wheels (in fact *particularly* if you think that). A 'visitor attraction' called Jorvik, the city's original name, makes much of the Viking origins of York. It promises streets as they would have been in AD975. So you come out with the plague and an arrow in your leg (that's a joke, but should New York really be New Jorvik?).

But York station itself is an absolute gem, with its huge, elegantly curved train shed dwarfing the trains inside. Look for the happy details, such as the company coat of arms in the spandrels in the roof supports (spandrels, some might need to know, are not naughty dogs but the flat bits between a pillar and an arch next to it). Less happy is the plaque beside one of the platforms marking the moment in the early hours of 29 April 1942, when a sister locomotive to the record-breaking *Mallard* mentioned opposite, the 4469 *Sir Ralph Wedgwood*, was destroyed by a German bomb in the so-called Baedeker Raids (Baedeker was a well-known brand of German guidebooks apparently used by the Germans

YORK STATION

RICHIE CHAN/DREAMSTIME.COM

during the war to help them make sneak attacks on picturesque ancient towns at night and bomb them without mercy or any military purpose).

YORK TO EDINBURGH***
TO THE WORLD'S FIRST RAILWAY
2HRS 40MINS, 205 MILES

Not long after York and despite the curious Zero milepost on Platform 4 at that station you can soon see the restored LNER sign on the right saying 'Edinburgh 200 miles'; it is followed not long afterwards by one saying, 'Edinburgh London halfway' and a bit further by one saying 'London 200 miles'. In fact, it is 393 miles by rail from King's Cross to Edinburgh Waverley, so if they'd made the route a few miles longer they could have had one sign not three!

Also, high up on the right, is a white horse carved into a hill, one of perhaps

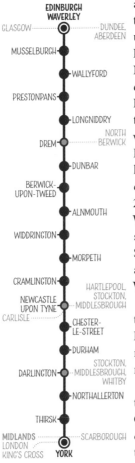

a dozen around Britain, some prehistoric. Consider the geography for a minute: we are racing north up the flat lands of the Vale of York. The White Horse is carved on the shoulder of the beautiful North York Moors (right), a set of hills that march east for not many miles to the North Sea at Whitby. Looking left (west) you can see the Pennine Hills, the backbone of England, with distant escarpments visible from the train, with the lovely Yorkshire Dales making those river valleys coming out of the hills – Wensleydale being the most obvious and cheesiest. So we are racing up a gap only about 20 miles wide to reach the Scottish border. The West Coast Main Line races north on the other side of the Pennines, almost touching the Irish Sea at Lancaster, but then hits the Cumbrian Hills at the Lake District and has a hefty climb to Shap. We, on the ECML, are on much the better route.

Only a madman would go up the middle along the Pennines – which is precisely what the Midland Railway did, beaten to the easier east and west coast routes, with its insanely ambitious Settle & Carlisle route in the hills to our left.

There are about ten former wartime airfields along this stretch, some still visible, mostly RAF Bomber Command, whose motto 'Strike hard, strike sure' came to have horrendous reality for Germany after those Baedeker Raids (mentioned on page 19).

We speed through the little town of **Thirsk** (home to *All Creatures Great and Small* author James Herriot, actually named Alf Wight – there's a museum to him on Kirkgate; 🖰 worldofjamesherriot.com).

Just after **Northallerton** (lovely High Street, good pubs, cafés and shops), where **NORTHALLERTON–EAGLESCLIFFE LINE** diverges, there is a pretty, isolated chapel on the left, near a village with the charming name Danby Wiske.

Soon we are under the roof at **Darlington** – again the spandrels of the roof supports are worth a look. Home of the world's very first powered public railway, the Stockton & Darlington of 1825 – on its opening day, George Stephenson's 'moveable engine' *Locomotion* did the nine-mile route in two hours. However, nearing the end of the trip he dramatically increased speed to 15mph. One passenger was so alarmed at this that he threw himself from the wagon and was badly injured.

In a Darlington park you can see evidence of the original track and its strange stone block sleepers. Fittingly, the first brand-new express steam locomotive made in Britain for many years, built by enthusiasts, was completed there in 2008: it is called *Tornado*. It's a beautiful machine and the boiler was made in Germany, where – the sad history of not many paragraphs before notwithstanding – the steam fans now have found many firm friends. For the Head of Steam Museum, change at Darlington to go one stop to North Road on the **BISHOP AUCKLAND LINE**. Or continue three stops further to Shildon for the Locomotion Museum. Both are recommended for rail enthusiasts.

From Darlington you can also take a particularly pretty route, the **ESK VALLEY LINE**, down to the sea at Whitby. You may have to change at Middlesbrough.

Just after the station is a curious church on the right with three arches in its squat tower, known as the Railwayman's Church, not just because railwaymen worship there but because the railway architect designed it.

Be alert about 12 miles later for one of this route's great treasures. After we see the 'London 250 miles' sign on the right, and we curve sharpish left and right into a bit of a cutting, we shoot through **Durham***** station (or much better, stop).

The view on the right after the station is peerless: Durham Castle and Cathedral sitting on their near-island in a loop in the River Wear. William the Conqueror realised he could create a near-impregnable seat of power here, and the view from the ten-arch railway viaduct is just superb.

As we pass through the little station of **Chester-le-Street** the striking and enormous sculpture *The Angel of the North* becomes visible on the right. Known locally as 'Rusty Rita' and resembling a human figure with aircraft wings, she stands beside the A1, which is yet again near our tracks.

Newcastle upon Tyne**, coming up, is fascinating and dramatic, so watch out. The River Tyne flows through a deep cut heading east, and the railways run at high level either side of this with junctions allowing us to leap across the river on a high bridge. The Tyne was immortalised for its five bridges in various songs, though of course there are now more, the oddest being the low-level, winking-eye millennium footbridge, which rotates to allow ships through (not while people are crossing it, one hopes).

There are castles and churches and weird modern buildings, some right next to the tracks and some across the river, and views down to quaysides. The thing like a huge mirrored pupa of an insect across the river (once we've crossed it) is the Sage Building, a Norman Foster design (the man who brought you the Gherkin in London). The weirdest thing I ever saw in Newcastle was a black cat painted with white stripes to match the Newcastle football strip: such cats are called 'Toon Cats' and, given cats' desire to keep clean, it is a cruel practice. Recommended side route: **TYNE VALLEY LINE** to Carlisle (61 miles) through the Tyne Valley.

Coming up is a real treat: one of the world's best train rides, but the first few miles after Newcastle are unexceptional, with a Traincare depot on the right. 'Traincare' evidently dates from the recent past when it was regarded as trendy to run English words together as if we were speaking German. In that language, I found *Lokomotivführer* an excellent word for train driver, or Norwegian *lokstall* is rather nice for engine shed, but I feel this habit is Orwellian in English, trying to disguise a fact with vagueness and a forced emotion. Thus the Railway Children's Home at Woking became 'Railcare'. Does that make it really more caring, or more meaningless? Actually it was originally called the London & South Western Railway Servants' Orphanage, which was at least accurate, informative and honest.

We pass through **Manors** (featured in the thriller *Get Carter*) and **Cramlington**. The coal workings around here extended for more than a mile under the North Sea, which we glimpse after passing a high viaduct at **Morpeth** and just before **Widdrington** station. Also on the right are two pillboxes, which remind us that even this far north the British feared invasion in 1940.

The fact that we have only just now glimpsed the sea after some 300 miles from London shows what a misnomer 'East Coast Main Line' has been so far. But we are about to make up for that, big time – unlike the poor souls on the even more misnamed 'West Coast Main Line', who glimpse the sea briefly near Lancaster and Carlisle then never again!

Here there are more rivers, and viaducts to cross them. One of the prettiest is soon reached at **Alnmouth****; the town is to the right by the river mouth. Local enthusiasts are rebuilding the short branch to Alnwick as the **ALN VALLEY RAILWAY**, but seem unlikely to link up towards the town itself because of the busy A1 road obliterating the old track. Shame. Put in a level crossing, lads, that'll learn 'em!

ALNWICK CASTLE

D K GROVE/SHUTTERSTOCK.COM

Alnwick Castle is home to the Dukes of Northumberland – the ancient Percy family, immortalised by Shakespeare with the 'Hotspur' character in *Henry IV*. The Percys make the current Windsors in Buckingham Palace seem like Johnnie-come-latelys; the castle and gardens are well worth a visit. Here – a link with both King's Cross and Glenfinnan – 14 flying Ford Anglias were crashed during the making of *Harry Potter and the Chamber of Secrets*, for the castle becomes Hogwarts in the movie. Or so I was told locally, perhaps by leg-pullers – weren't they computer generated?

Now concentrate on the views to the right. Here you can see the fabulous 'Holy Island' of Lindisfarne, cradle of Christianity in the north, and linked to the mainland by a tidal causeway, obviously visible more clearly at low tide with its refuge tower. At the island's south end (right, looking across) there is a village, a castle on its low, grassy mound, and several homes made from upturned, tarred-black boats with chimneys and windows cut in their hulls (like those described in Charles Dickens's *David Copperfield*). The rather sinister-looking pair of obelisks on the right are leading marks, directing boats for the best channel to approach from the sea. Further to the right (south of Lindisfarne) is the stunningly located Bamburgh Castle. The railway viewpoint just couldn't be better.

The Lindisfarne causeway is cut off for around four hours around each high tide. It causes no end of fun with stuck campervans, strange effects on

THE EXTRAORDINARY SAGA OF
FLYING SCOTSMAN & THE FLYING SCOTSMAN

Every day since 1862, *The Flying Scotsman* has sped between King's Cross and Edinburgh. True, the train at the start was officially called the *Special Scotch Express* and took 10½ hours, but at some point the nickname *The Flying Scotsman* took hold. 'The Race to the North' railway rivalry of 1888 (see box, page 78) ended with this service speeded up to 8½ hours.

By the 1920s, with private cars and airlines eating into the railways' dominance, the new London and North Eastern Railway (LNER), decided on a daring move. It introduced a new class of loco, led by one confusingly called *Flying Scotsman*. These brainchildren of genius Nigel Gresley could run non-stop the nearly 400 miles between the capital cities because of the powerful design, and a tiny corridor under the coal tender by which the crew could be replaced mid-journey, plus the scooping up of water from long troughs between the rails.

In the 1930s, the time fell to 7 hours 20 minutes, while levels of luxury rose, with an onboard hairdressing salon, restaurants, cocktail bars and secretaries for businessmen. The year 1962 saw the introduction of the enormously powerful Deltic diesels and the time came down to 6 hours, then with better track to 5 hours 20 minutes. In 1978, the 125mph High Speed Train arrived and did King's Cross to Edinburgh in just 4 hours 35 minutes. In 1991, the route was electrified – in British Railways' last big effort before privatisation – and today *The Flying Scotsman* takes under 4½ hours, less than half the original journey time.

Meanwhile, what happened to the steam locomotive by the same name? Scrapped like her forlorn sisters?

Well, no, and it was all down to a small boy who climbed up on the footplate of *Flying Scotsman* at the British Empire Exhibition in 1924. The lad in short trousers and grey socks was one Alan Pegler. He was overawed by the beauty of the gleaming, almost brand-new machine with her flawless apple-green paintwork.

As Alan Pegler grew up he heard of her record exploits – first non-stop run in 1928, first authenticated 100mph by a steam loco in 1934. Then came the war years and she was stripped of her glamour, and, dirty black, used to pull any old train.

By 1963 with diesels taking over, she was heading for the cutting torch in the scrapyard, like all 76 of her sister locos. In stepped a now wealthy businessman, the same Alan Pegler. He paid £3,000 for the loco and somehow won running rights on the network – by 1968 she ended up being the only steam loco allowed to run on the main lines.

Having re-enacted her famous non-stop run to Edinburgh, Pegler took *Flying Scotsman* for a tour of the USA. But governments changed, the Vietnam War was raging and with the Troubles flaring into warfare in Northern Ireland, some Irish Americans seemed to threaten the British locomotive's tour of the States. The tour was going to be a failure.

But Pegler had promised to deliver some historic carriages to a museum, and honoured the deal at his own expense. He did it and went bust. Again she seemed doomed. American creditors wanted her, and Pegler hid *Flying Scotsman* in a West Coast air base.

TONY MARSH, VISITSCOTLAND

Yet again, a miracle happened to save No 4472. Sir William McAlpine – yes, a relative of 'Concrete Bob' McAlpine who built the Mallaig line (see box, page 127) – bought her, shipped her back through the Panama Canal and repaired her, with the help of Pete Waterman, the pop producer and rail fan. She started her touring career again, taking in a trip to Australia where in 1988 she broke another record – the world's longest non-stop steam run.

In 2004, at long last *Flying Scotsman* was bought for the nation, with the help of another knight, Sir Richard Branson. She was restored yet again, this time at the National Railway Museum, and no-one was more pleased than one grey-whiskered old man in a wheelchair, Alan Pegler (who also helped save the Ffestiniog Railway in the Welsh mountains). He was honoured with an OBE in 2006 (a knighthood would have been better).

Pegler died in 2012. At his funeral, as his coffin left the congregation, a recording of *Flying Scotsman* being driven away by him into the distance in the echoing American hills was played, slowly fading away to silence.

At some point in this tangled saga of the most-travelled loco in the world, amateurs were allowed to drive *Flying Scotsman* in the Midlands as a fundraiser. I leapt at the chance.

Climbing up on to that hallowed footplate, I gingerly pulled the regulator handle down just about the width of a 2p coin: 135 tons of steel, coal, water and steam – and not an ounce of electronics or computers – leapt forward like a Mini Cooper. The power available was immense, I realised, as I blew that famous whistle for a crossing. For just a moment, it was like being allowed to play on Wimbledon Centre Court and win. Wow!

Years later I heard some expert say: 'And did you know in the 1980s some fool let amateurs drive *Flying Scotsman* up and down a track in the Midlands? What were they thinking of? Like using Concorde as a dodgem car. Bloody idiots!'

'Absolutely, tut tut. Bloody idiots,' I murmured. Bet he never drove *Flying Scotsman*.

the tide coming down from the north, and supposedly strange effects on the opening hours in the island's pubs. Well, legend has it anyway, about past publicans at least – how was the local cop going to get across once the tide was up?

Soon another real treat comes up, with **Berwick-upon-Tweed*****. Look out for the Tweedmouth Lighthouse. Passing that small town, which is across the river from Berwick, look ahead for a fine view of the Royal Border Bridge.

In fact three bridges cross this handsome river, which traverses much of the Scottish Borders (and indeed is the border for most of its course). There's the magnificent railway bridge we are purring across (the *Royal Border Bridge*, 28 arches, built by Robert Stephenson, son of George, see page 21), the modern road bridge and a more ancient bridge below. Before that was built, there were ferries.

Berwick has famously changed hands a few times. It once came to be at war with Russia for more than a century by accident, with the Soviet Union sending an ambassador to sue for peace between Berwick and Moscow.

It's decidedly English now, and after the station you get a glimpse of the massive fortifications necessary to stop the kilted chaps grabbing it back. Just after that, you cross the border.

No route into Scotland can compare with that of *The Flying Scotsman*: the **ASTONISHING BEAUTY** of Berwick revealed suddenly as the train comes over the cliffs… the three great bridges, each a **MASTERPIECE** of its day – and as the train slows and enters upon the loftiest of the three, Robert Stephenson's Royal Border Bridge, the passenger on *The Flying Scotsman* surveying this fair scene and watching his motoring friends below… has as J J Bell once expressed it 'the advantage of the eagle over the sparrow'.
The late, **GREAT** railway writer, O S Nock

We now climb the cliffs towards Eyemouth (where fishermen have a Herring Queen every year) and get superb sea views. Then it's inland through some hills, still dogged by the A1 heading for the same prize, and you can see the Scottish mileposts are now counting down towards Edinburgh.

Just after milepost 43, you see another one of those huge LNER signs, this one saying 'London 350 miles'. We get our first glimpse of the Fife coast to the north, looking way across the Firth of Forth. New stations at Reston and East Linton, before and after Dunbar respectively, should be built along here soon.

Just after milepost 29 we whizz through **Dunbar****; look out for a superb view of the island of Bass Rock, and flat Fidra beyond. On the right, what looks like a mine slag heap in its conical shape is Berwick Law, a volcanic 'crag and tail' left scraped clean by glaciers after the last ice age. You can spot others in the landscape, particularly the one Edinburgh Castle sits on.

ABOVE EDINBURGH WAVERLEY STATION

KENNY LAM, VISITSCOTLAND

Behind Berwick Law – law is Scottish for 'hill' – lies North Berwick, as pretty a little seaside resort as you could hope for, reached from Edinburgh in about half an hour by the **NORTH BERWICK LINE** which joins us at **Drem** (see page 62 for the North Berwick excursion from Edinburgh). On a clear day you can see two hills in Fife (known as the 'Paps o' Fife') across the sea to the right. All of this gazing northwards might stop us seeing a fine pillar of a monument to the south (our left) about a mile away on a hill. It is one of two similar Hopetoun monuments (see Springfield in Fife, page 73).

Shortly afterwards, just before **Longniddry**, is a sandstone castle ruin on the right.

Now we can see the hills of Fife across the Forth more clearly, and exciting occasional glimpses of Edinburgh Castle and Arthur's Seat (Edinburgh's highest hill) ahead, as well as glimpses of the Forth Bridge beyond. As we whistle through **Prestonpans**, **Wallyford** and **Musselburgh** (next to the new

For further adventures on the **EAST COAST MAIN LINE** see page 67.

27

THE BEST THINGS TO DO IN EDINBURGH

You don't visit Edinburgh: you fall in love with the place. It's a spectacular setting, but it's simple too. Two parallel streets go east–west high up either side of the railway which runs in a deep valley, each getting on for a mile long. That's it, basically! To the north is Princes Street and then behind it the Georgian splendour and grid-pattern orderliness of the New Town, bending over the hill to give glimpses of the Firth of Forth. Shopaholics' paradise Princes Street, closer to the railway, is staked out at each end by the Balmoral and Caledonian former railway hotels, with the mad Gothic spaceship (my description!) of the Scott Monument part way down. Good landmarks, but don't ignore Waterloo Place carrying on up to Calton Hill at the east end.

To the south – what a Jekyll and Hyde contrast, and that book was written by an Edinburgh-born man! – is the Royal Mile, with many a medieval and spooky tale to tell. If you want stories of witches, grave-robbing, ghosts, hidden streets, plague, executions and all that, 'Auld Reekie' as this city was known, is the best place. The Royal Mile ascends from the Palace of Holyroodhouse in the east – where you can also find the newish Scottish Parliament (opened in 1999 after a brief adjournment... from 1707!) – up to magnificent Edinburgh Castle in the west. Two roads link these very different key streets across the railway – the Mound (which has the National Gallery on it) and North Bridge, which dramatically leaps across Waverley station. That's it with the orientation but the up and down of it all means is that everywhere you turn in Edinburgh you get a different view, always interesting, sometimes sensational, aided by more creative architectural genius than you could ever think possible. Here in brief are a few highlights for visitors:

Note: Edinburgh gets very, very busy during the summer Festival Fringe and Hogmanay (New Year's Eve and a bit either side). Just make sure you have accommodation booked. If you're stuck, why not commute in by train from the many towns half an hour away?

ARTHUR'S SEAT Can you think of many capital cities where you can walk high up in a wilderness in the middle of it? With 360-degree views? It is a major climb up a serious hill and you need stout footwear and weather protection. Curiously, the hill has a Radical Road on one side and an Innocent Railway, too (more on page 112).

ROYAL YACHT BRITANNIA (Ocean Drive Ocean Terminal, EH6 6JJ ☎ 0131 555 5566 🖱 royalyachtbritannia.co.uk) This beautiful and well-kept ship at Leith docks is of historical importance, but didn't last as long in service as HM Queen Elizabeth II, whose refuge it was. Her first global tour as Queen was on a different ship since HMY *Britannia* had not yet been

Queen Margaret University campus) we can soon see Calton Hill, through which our train will tunnel. It is covered with fascinating monuments and absolutely worth the climb from the station for the best view of Edinburgh.

I can't here detail everything that's great about Edinburgh (see the box above for my suggestions on what to see and do), but as you reach **Edinburgh**

built. It was in service from 1954 until 1997, but after the yacht was retired – let's not enter the argument over whether that was really necessary or politically mean-minded – the monarch herself sailed on for decades more. One Cornish doctor visiting remarked to me: 'It's curious how Spartan it is.' Exactly. If you are born to palaces, castles and grand dinners for 2,000 – what do you want for escape? Something quiet, simple, private and unfussy, I imagine.

THE ROYAL MILE Well, with the castle at one end and the palace at the other, there are so many things in between. Boswell Court is worth a peek, there's the Camera Obscura and World of Illusions, Museum of Childhood and St Giles Cathedral, plus more tartanalia than Rod Stewart's *trooser* collection, and whisky galore. Nice for a poke around.

CALTON HILL I think this is the best view in town, plus it's free and within walking distance of Waverley station. To be honest, if you haven't got the time or stamina for Arthur's Seat, this is a corker of a view too, and is home to several fascinating monuments. Don't miss the Old Calton Burial Ground on the way down – beautiful, and equally fascinating.

EDINBURGH CASTLE (Castlehill, EH1 2NG ☎ 0131 668 8956 📱 edinburghcastle. scot) Jammed full of historical interest, but don't jump out of your skin if the artillery starts firing: it's not the Jacobite rebellion restarting. Well at least not if it's one o'clock when the signal gun fires, originally for the benefit of setting clocks and chronometers, or just timing your daily routine – a sort of 18th-century Apple Watch, but too large and noisy to be worn on the wrist. (If it's not 1pm, it probably *is* the Jacobites, or the English.) Don't miss tiny St Margaret's Chapel (she was normal size, it's the church that is small), Mons Meg (a huge gun, love the name), the National War Museum, the Honours of Scotland (crown jewels) and the much-travelled Stone of Destiny, which sounds so *Game of Thrones*, doesn't it? In fact, that's what it was and is – with real thrones.

NATIONAL MUSEUM OF SCOTLAND (Chambers St, EH1 1JF ☎ 0300 123 6789 📱 nms.ac.uk/Scotland) Love this building, and you are guaranteed to find fascinating stories in its storeys. Great views from the top, too.

GREAT DAYS OUT BY TRAIN This book details fab fun excursions from the capital such as to the seaside at charming North Berwick (page 62), to the lovely Borders at Tweedbank (page 110), and to Fife (taking in the famed Forth Bridge, twice; page 72).

Waverley*** station, the Old Town and castle are high on the left, and Princes Street, the New Town and the Scott Monument are high on the right. Indeed, Scott's Waverley novels gave the station its name. If you are a first-timer, you have a treat in store! If you are a repeat visitor, you'll already love the place.

KENNY LAM, VISITSCOTLAND

KENNY LAM, VISITSCOTLAND

KENNY LAM, VISITSCOTLAND

KENNY LAM, VISITSCOTLAND

1 Arthur's Seat **2** Scott Monument **3** Royal Yacht Britannia **4** National Museum of Scotland **5** The approach to Edinburgh Castle along Castle Esplanade **6** Colourful Victoria Street – often cited as as J K Rowling's inspiration for Diagon Alley **7** Greyfriars Bobby

GETTING TO GLASGOW*
THE WEST COAST MAIN LINE
4HRS 50MINS, 399 MILES

Of the admittedly very fast and useful West Coast Main Line (WCML), which goes all the way from London Euston to Glasgow, the only really great bit scenically is Lancaster to Carlisle. Here we zoom up the Lune Gorge alongside the M6 motorway, with views of the Pennines to the east, and the Lake District mountains to the west; the summit comes at Shap, 916ft. Look out for a terrific but redundant viaduct joining from your right before this. This can, by the way, be combined with other routes to make great days out (eg: Settle & Carlisle, Cumbrian Coast Line).

The problem is that you don't really see much west coast on the West Coast (a glimpse at Lancaster). Thus this book recommends, and devotes much more space to, arriving from London on the far more interesting East Coast Main Line. Euston, we have a problem!

Having said that, Carlisle, just over the border into England, is a fascinating place (see box, opposite). And not only does the WCML link Manchester and Birmingham and towns in between straight to Glasgow this way, but Carlisle being a hub offers much more imaginative routes. For instance, coming from, or going to, Leeds: make a day of it. Go over the wonderful **SETTLE & CARLISLE LINE***** (England's answer to the West Highland in Scotland) and take a break here (the S&C is fully described in our companion book, *Britain from the Rails: A Window Gazer's Guide*).

Then, if you are not in a great hurry, don't whizz up the almost station-less WCML to Glasgow Central but arrive there via the more scenic **GLASGOW AND SOUTH-WESTERN**** route through Dumfries (page 81). Or, one day, take the even lovelier Borders Railway through Hawick and Melrose to Edinburgh – not yet, it's only been partly rebuilt and reopened (see that part on page 107). But I'll be on the first train right through, that I promise!

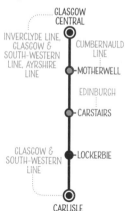

GLASGOW CENTRAL

INVERCLYDE LINE, GLASGOW & SOUTH-WESTERN LINE, AYRSHIRE LINE

CUMBERNAULD LINE

MOTHERWELL

EDINBURGH

CARSTAIRS

GLASGOW & SOUTH-WESTERN LINE

LOCKERBIE

CARLISLE

CARLISLE TO GLASGOW*
1HR 11MINS, 102 MILES

If you do go straight up the WCML to Glasgow from Carlisle, the only station in the Borders hills is **Lockerbie.** I say Borders – it's actually in Dumfries and Galloway, but you get the idea. Once upon a time there was also a nice, quiet country railway from here direct to Dumfries – I say nice, quiet, but in 1883 they managed to have a serious accident here with a train coming off the branch and hitting a goods train *and* a Glasgow express, but that's a long while ago. Such an accident is not possible nowadays, particularly as the branch line's long been Beeching-ed away.

The oddest thing about Lockerbie, as I wrote this at any rate, is that it was staffed and run by the national operator, ScotRail, but none of its trains ever called there, which makes it unique in Scotland. The West Coast expresses stopped once or twice during the day, but mainly it was the Trans-Pennine Express services going from Manchester Airport to Glasgow (usefully, an all-electric route) with an hourly service.

Beyond this (going towards Glasgow) the next station is, or rather was, Beattock, which surely deserves to reopen when you consider all the nearby towns and villages, such as adjoining Moffat. Locals complain that this 48-mile stretch from Lockerbie to Carstairs is the longest without a station in Britain and I fully support their campaign to get the stop reopened.

LONG MEMORIES AT CARLISLE

Carlisle Citadel station, built in Tudor-Gothic style, had no fewer than seven railway companies operating over eight routes at one time – the most of any British station – and even today it has several companies operating six routes radiating either side of the border. It has three long platforms for through trains and three short bays facing north and south, all used.

Busy? A recent pre-Covid Wednesday saw 169 passenger and 84 freight trains pass through, and at night this includes four very long sleeping-car trains.

There are plenty of odd details to look out for. Some are obvious – the gargoyles on the tower, the strange circles in the main inside roof trusses, the coats of arms on the front, or the Tudor arches (and no, that's not another gargoyle, it's that irate guard from the Dumfries train leaning out of a window).

There's something odd in the square outside the station: not the actual cannon used to repel Bonnie Prince Charlie's army, proudly displayed at the top of English Street, but less obvious. Tucked away by the archway on the right of the square is a curious blue enamel sign, saying: 'London Midland & Scottish Railway: Private Road and/or footpath.' I hope some thieving magpie hasn't whipped it by the time you get there. This company ceased to exist in 1948, but its notices still warn you of things.

Mind you, railwaymen tend to have even older memories. They still refer to the various routes from here in nicknames that recall companies before even the LMS was formed in 1923: 'The Caley', 'the Lanky', 'the M&C', 'the Cumbrian' or 'the Sou'western'. Or so I was told … As if to confirm this, when I left on a train south, the lettering on a long building on the right announced 'Maryport & Carlisle Railway Goods Depot', one of those early companies that ceased to exist in 1923. Now that *is* old.

Just beyond is **Beattock Summit**, the steep climb up to it made famous by W H Auden's poem *Night Mail* (page 174). It required banking locos shoving at your back buffers in the days of steam (don't we all on these hills!) but today's electrics glide up as if the hill isn't there. Nonetheless, it is a 1,016ft-above-sea-level summit, a sign tells us, and it is 52 miles from Glasgow and 349 miles from London.

Speeding on, downhill now into the Clyde's rainfall catchment area, we whizz through miles of station-less but scenic countryside – using the lean

TEN TERRIFIC THINGS TO SEE & DO IN GLASGOW

The modern cliché 'vibrant' doesn't do Glasgow justice (and let's be honest, it's always applied to places that aren't. No-one says 'vibrant Paris', or 'vibrant New York', do they? It's always somewhere like 'vibrant Stevenage'. Ditto 'city of culture' – they usually give that to somewhere that hasn't got any, not Venice). Glasgow's a lot more than vibrant. Buzzing with energy: myriad arts and entertainment, brilliant bars and restaurants, perennially young at heart, both radical and conservative at once. Here's just a few suggestions:

KELVINGROVE ART GALLERY & MUSEUM (Argyle St, G3 8AG ☎ 0141 276 9599 ♿ glasgowlife.org.uk/museums) Great rainy-day option: 22 galleries, 8,000 objects, something for everyone, worth a couple of hours. Free. Nearest station: Partick.

THE BURRELL COLLECTION (Pollokshaws Rd, Pollok Country Park, G43 1AT ♿ glasgowlife. org.uk/museums) A sensational private and eclectic collection given to the city by Glasgow's Getty, Sir William Burrell, a wealthy shipping magnate. Closed for renovation at the time of writing (pre-Covid), but will be worth it again when they fix the leaky roof. Not suitable for a rainy day until then! Nearest station: Pollokshaws West.

POLLOK HOUSE (Pollokshaws Rd, Pollok Country Park, G43 1AT ☎ 0141 616 6410 ♿ nts.org.uk/visit/places/pollok-house) Near the Burrell, impressive collection of Spanish art, as well as works by Raeburn and Guthrie, brilliant formal gardens, plus *Downton Abbey*-style servants' quarters (more on page 54). Nearest station: Pollokshaws West.

SHARMANKA KINETIC THEATRE (103 Trongate, G1 5HD ☎ 0141 552 7080 ♿ sharmanka.com) Hundreds of carved figures and pieces of old junk and scrap, assembled by eccentric Russians, perform an incredible choreography to haunting music and synchronised light, telling the funny and tragic stories of the human spirit. Described by one visitor as 'a fantasy toy shop come to life'. Children? Rainy day? Yep! Nearest station: Argyle Street (but walking distance of both main termini).

GLASGOW SCHOOL OF ART (167 Renfrew St, G3 6RQ ☎ 0141 353 4500 ♿ gsaarchives. net) Although it has suffered two serious fires in recent years (2014 and 2018), by the time you read this, I hope Glasgow School of Art will be back to its former glory. They are sure to take more care of the heritage of wonderful

on the trains or track to cope with the many curves – to reach, 33 minutes from Lockerbie, **Carstairs**, an important junction where lines to Edinburgh and Glasgow diverge. Sleeper trains divide here and East Coast Main Line expresses can and do reach Glasgow because of a curve connecting the two arms of the 'Y'.

We speed on through little stations such as **Carluke**, with wide views of the Clyde Valley and the hills of Lanarkshire and Ayrshire, and **Motherwell**

Scots architect/designer/artist Charles Rennie Mackintosh. Almost everyone likes his turn-of-the-20th-century style – on the cusp of Art Nouveau and Art Deco somehow. It might be tastier if you go to the lovely Willow Tearooms, designed by Mackintosh for patron Miss Kate Cranston. There is also a pretty good replica Willow Tea Rooms nearby (see below). Nearest station: Central.

BUCHANAN STREET If you like all the designer big names, this is the place for a spot of retail therapy. And if you shop till you drop, some great eateries too (including the aforementioned tea room). Particularly lovely at Christmas. Nearest station: between Central and Queen Street, so hard to miss. And nearby is:

GEORGE SQUARE A bit of landmark grandeur suggesting what an important role the 'second city of the British Empire' once had. Nearest station: Glasgow Queen Street is on one corner.

THE RIVERSIDE MUSEUM OF TRANSPORT & TRAVEL (100 Pointhouse Pl, G3 8RS ☎ 0141 287 2720w 📱 glasgowlife.org.uk/museums) With its wacky zig-zag roof – maybe they made one three times too big

and had to squash it up! – this is a Glasgow landmark. The front is just the beginning of a quite amazing building. And to be serious, it's a great roof and at least it didn't leak, like a certain other art collection building in Glasgow. Inside you'll find locomotives, trams, old sailing ships, vintage cars and lots of interactive stuff for children. Nearest station: Partick.

NECROPOLIS (50 Cathedral Sq, G4 0UZ ☎ 0141 287 5064 📱 glasgownecropolis.org) Dead centre of Glasgow, the old joke goes, but in fact a fascinating place to ramble round on a par with Paris's Père-Lachaise. Great views of the cathedral. One of those areas where you'd get even more out of it with a walking tour. If you are going to the Necropolis it's also worth visiting the oldest house in Glasgow nearby on Castle Street: Provands Lordship, built in 1471. Nearest station: High Street. Or just walk east from Glasgow Queen Street a few streets.

FOOTBALL STADIA If you're a die-hard fanatical footie fan, these are a must. There's a beautiful building for the beautiful game at Ibrox, to take just one example, and excellent tours. But Hampden Park and Celtic Park are the stuff of legends, too.

1 Glasgow Necropolis **2** The iconic landmark that is George Square **3** Pollok House is home to an impressive collection of Spanish art **4** Floating heads at Kelvingrove Art Gallery **5** The Riverside Museum of Transport and Travel (where many trains do stop; change for various suburban services including a line to Cumbernauld). Then it's on through Glasgow suburbs and over the Clyde into the bustling big-city grandeur of **Glasgow Central**.

WHAT CAN YOU SPY WITH THE GLASGOW CENTRAL INTELLIGENCE AGENCY?

Much the busiest and yet the nicest in the city, Glasgow Central is a brilliant station well worth a visit (also enthused about on page 38). Note the elegant elliptical dark wooden shop shapes and their restrained lettering, and the huge wartime shell used as a charity collecting box near one main entrance, and a curious mosaic at the other. The Grand Central Hotel, facing the departure boards, is well worth a cheeky visit for its *Queen Mary*-era styling (that is resembling the interior of the ship, built just up the road at the same time, not the grumpy old queen).

Grand Central Hotel has played host to all kinds of showbiz royalty: Sinatra, The Beatles, Laurel and Hardy (and somewhat differently, Hitler's Deputy, Rudolf Hess, supposedly got on a train from Platform 1 after he was arrested in Scotland in 1941). Try the champagne bar, even if you are staying somewhere cheaper – the Rennie Mackintosh Hotel also adjoins the station on the east side and while not so many stars, may be a lot less costly.

If the weather's bearable, it's worth a stroll down by the river to the contrasting elegant footbridges just up and just down river from the railway bridge, making a loop. You can see how busy the rail bridge is while you do this – I could see four trains at once moving on it – and also some empty bridge piers along the east side. Those old piers align with the original 1879 station (the low numbered platforms on the east side), whereas the newer bridge lines up with the newer 1901 part of the station, to the west and nearer the river. So the old station tracks swerve to line up with the newer, stronger bridge. But those old piers – wait a minute – are those words carved on the granite?

Yes, but it may be hard to make out the detail unless the sun is shining sideways. They say, in Greek and English: 'All greatness stands firm in the storm.' Good slogan for bridge piers, even if they are redundant. This is a public artwork by Ian Hamilton Finlay, not your usual mindless graffito on railway bridges, but is a line from Plato, no less. But then a city should be judged by its piers.

There is also a nearby figure of La Pasionaria, the symbolic heroine of the 1930s Spanish Civil War, a conflict which many idealistic Scots joined – and some never returned from. Both monuments seem to epitomise elements of this bustling city, once dubbed 'the second city of the Empire' – love of public art, a lot of redundant industrial history, and socialist or humanist idealism.

Bradt on
BRITAIN

Bradt GUIDES
TRAVEL TAKEN SERIOUSLY

bradtguides.com/shop

The Kelpies, Falkirk (KENNY LAM, VISIT SCOTLAND)

THE CENTRAL BELT

EDINBURGH *AND* GLASGOW

With no fewer than five possible rail routes between Scotland's two greatest cities, and the lines electrified and, in some cases, done in less than an hour, you might miss some gems absolutely worth stopping off to visit. Here's a guide to the lines and the dozens of towns and villages they serve.

GLASGOW TO EDINBURGH VIA FALKIRK**

THE QUICKEST & BEST ROUTE
45MINS, 42 MILES

The Edinburgh and Glasgow Railway was opened in 1842 as the first line between Scotland's two biggest cities – there are now five – and is still considered the main route, being the fastest. It's only worth maintaining one for tip-top high-speed running, so use this unless you want access to places on other routes.

I'd sit on the north side (left coming from Glasgow, which is what I'll describe here).

THE ROUTE DESCRIBED

After leaving **Glasgow Queen Street** up a steep tunnel on this line, there's a big rail triangle on the right (*Cowlairs South* and *West Jns*) and the *Eastfield depot*. There is a plan to insert an extra suburban station about two miles down the track, but for the time being the first one is **Bishopbriggs** (3¼ miles), served only by suburban services to Croy and Stirling, so we probably won't stop. A plaque recalls local hero Thomas Muir, 'father of Scottish democracy' who campaigned for reform in the 1790s. But as for today, because the charming original station was replaced by some dull modern effort, speeding through is not so bad. This station featured in the 1980 film *That Sinking Feeling*, but that certainly isn't a comment on this friendly place!

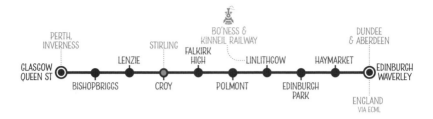

Lenzie (6¼ miles) comes next, but this is also normally whizzed through, so our first possible stop is at **Croy** (11½ miles). Some expresses don't bother to stop here either. This station is where the stopping suburban services peel off left (north) to Stirling, finishing at either Alloa or Dunblane, so residents of Croy and the area benefit from at least four trains an hour to Glasgow (two on the Edinburgh–Glasgow services, two on the Stirling–Glasgow line) and up to eight in peak times.

Next we cross over the M80 Motorway and then over the **CUMBERNAULD LINE** (page 49), another rail route between Edinburgh and Glasgow. A junction soon lets trains from our line join that one, and we can see that

ANTONINE WALL & THE RIGHT TO ROME

On Croy Hill, to the northeast of the village of the same name, are some remains of the Romans' Antonine Wall, a northern version of the more famous Hadrian's Wall, to which the legionaries retreated. This one was built between AD142 and 144, including a fort and two beacon platforms. Much of our route today has earthworks from the Antonine Wall, including Falkirk.

It is a source of pride to some present-day Scots that their predecessors saw off the mighty Roman Army. A humorous story told by Scots goes like this. The Romans are approaching when a Pict (from the local tribe) rushes out and shouts at them, waves his spear, bares his bottom and goes back over the hill. A Centurion is told to take 100 men and go over the hill and teach the barbarian a lesson. An hour later just three men return, clothes torn, wounded, weapons broken. 'What on earth happened?' asks the commander.

'There were two of them,' says the dejected Centurion.

Well, ho ho – what a bunch of Croy babies! – but if the Romans did stop around here and go back, you have to wonder why.

The one pitched battle between Rome and the Caledonian tribes in fact ended in a massacre of the locals. Agricola triumphed around AD83 at the Battle of Mons Graupius – today known as the Grampian Mountains – when perhaps 10,000 tribal warriors are thought to have died at the hands of a well-disciplined Roman legion of around half the size. But it wasn't that simple. The pugnacious Caledonians did not give up the struggle, but resorted to guerrilla war. One has to ask what was in it for Rome, to conquer the Highlands, where there seemed little to gain. At the same time there were defeats around the Danube and Rhine, which urgently needed troops transferred to those areas.

electrified line diverge to the left. On a decent day there are wonderful views of the hills to the left, across the valley.

Falkirk High follows – it is one of three stations serving that town, the others being Falkirk Grahamston and Camelon on the main line from Edinburgh to Perth and Stirling, which we join before the next stop at Polmont (making a giant triangle, with Croy the opposite corner). Falkirk High is indeed higher up than the other stations, and has on the Edinburgh-bound platform a whimsical sculpture 'Antonine the Legendary Engine' by the late George Wyllie, commissioned to commemorate the 150th anniversary of this line. *Falkirk High Tunnel* (774m) follows. The parallel Union Canal also goes into its own Falkirk Tunnel at this point, which is Scotland's longest and has the macabre distinction of being dug out by a workforce including two Irishmen, Burke and Hare, who went on to become mass murderers supplying Edinburgh's lucrative medical school anatomy trade. They followed that city's dubious tradition of grave robbing, but thought to cut out the middleman, as it were. Our tunnel, thankfully, has no such spooky connections.

Historian and archaeologist David Breeze comments perceptively: 'Perhaps if the tribes had not been so warlike, the mountains so high, the lack of economic benefit so obvious, geographical and social difficulties so great, Rome might have triumphed.' In fact, such were the pressures on the Roman Empire, they abandoned the whole of Britain by about 409 (thus just missing the 410 from Glasgow Queen Street!).

Coming back to railways, there is a connection with the ancient world. The standard gauge of railways worldwide (the 4ft 8½in between the track), which was settled after a huge battle in Britain in the 19th century and subsequently used in most countries, was perhaps decided by a Roman horse's bum. George Stephenson, who built the first proper railway in 1825, wanted his tracks to take the existing horse-drawn rail wagons from mine workings. Their width was decided by how far apart the wheels have to be to be outside the bearings that are outside the shafts that must be outside the horse pulling the thing. If you don't believe it, check the distance between Roman chariot wheels. They are pretty close to 4ft 8½in and, with flanges on, some of them could have run into Edinburgh Waverley station.

In fact, it probably goes back further than the Romans. What was thought to be an early Greek standard-gauge railway by excited archaeologists turned out to be stone wagonways with the ruts worn into a very regular groove, again at around 4ft 8½in spacing. Maybe it wasn't the Romans, then. The first man ever to make a decent chariot in ancient Sumeria or wherever decided the track gauge of the East Coast Main Line.

FALKIRK & LINLITHGOW: 'CRACKPOT' CONTRAPTION & BIRTHPLACE OF A DYNASTY

Touring Scotland by rail, you might enjoy visiting two rather special towns in the Central Belt, each with superb places to visit. Falkirk, roughly halfway between Edinburgh and Glasgow, has some wonderful, indeed world-class, attractions, but they are well spaced apart from either Falkirk High (FKK) or Falkirk Grahamston (FKG). You need to hire a bike, take buses or taxis, or be prepared for long walks. They are worth it. Linlithgow, on the other hand, offers a more concentrated set of sights within a short walk of the station, which has twice as many trains as either Falkirk option (because both routes from Glasgow to Edinburgh have joined together by then – eight trains an hour).

THE FALKIRK WHEEL (Lime Rd, FK1 4RS ☎ 0870 050 0208 ✆ scottishcanals.co.uk/falkirk-wheel) This apparently crackpot contraption is said to be the world's only rotating boat lift, which is, in fact, brilliantly effective and raises or lowers boats 35m between two canals once joined by a flight of locks (which have since become derelict). Got to be seen to be believed, and you can sometimes ride on it by taking a boat trip too. To get there, it's a short taxi ride or take the No 6 bus from the town centre. If you're feeling adventurous (stout shoes, stout heart and

head torch required), you can also reach it on foot – as both canals are near the two stations on their different lines, you simply have to follow them west (about 2½ miles) to where, by definition, they meet. The Forth and Clyde Canal runs a little north and west of FKG, the Union Canal is just south of FKK.

THE KELPIES AT HELIX PARK (The Helix, FK2 7ZT ☎ 01324 590600 ✆ thehelix.co.uk) Said to be the world's largest equestrian sculptures are the two amazing, gigantic horses' heads at the new Helix Park, two miles north of FKG, three miles from FKK. They are set next to a new extension of the Forth and Clyde Canal. Dramatic, stunning, but not so easy to reach except by taxi, bike or on foot.

CALLENDAR HOUSE (Callendar Park, FK1 1YR ☎ 01324 503770 ✆ falkirkcommunitytrust. org/venues/callendar-house) Explore 600 years of history, including the building of the French-château style mansion, set in Callendar Park, which is more easily walkable from either station than the attractions above.

LINLITHGOW PALACE (Kirkgate, EH49 7AL ☎ 01506 842896 ✆ historicenvironment. scot) Clearly visible from the railway (on the left coming from Glasgow, turn left down

But in 1984 there was bad news here on the railway a little further on, just before the junction with the main line going from Edinburgh to the north. An escaped cow caused a serious derailment. It showed the folly of pushing light carriages at high speed with a heavy locomotive at the back – an arrangement then being used to speed up the Glasgow–Edinburgh shuttles – (and without a Wild West-style cowcatcher, sadly). Today's trains avoid this danger, so don't worry.

the main street coming out of the station) is this impressive ruined palace with plenty of Mary Queen of Scots history (guided tours recommended). She was born here in 1542 and became queen as an infant – a fact that kicked off a whole turbulent era for Scotland, which ended with her imprisonment and execution by her cousin, Elizabeth of England in 1587 (who never actually met Mary). The building, although burned out in 1746, is still sensational and was clearly as good a palace as you would find around Europe at the time. It's set on a natural hill overlooking the loch, which has a good walking path around it, on the far side from the railway station. Admission charge for the palace, not the loch and grounds.

In front of the palace is the church of St Michael with its rather astonishing aluminium crown spire (that is an open spire). The original was the traditional open crown shape in stone (as you may see from the railway at Paisley) but had to be dismantled as it was in danger of collapsing. This 1960s one is considerably lighter, but make your own mind up about whether it suits the church (well worth a look around when open).

Note the glorious cross in the square, surrounded by fine buildings, as you approach. There's a statue of St Michael, too, and indeed the town's motto is 'St. Michael is kinde to straingers'. Judging by the welcome I received at the palace and pub, still true.

CANAL EXPLORATION As at Falkirk High, to the south of the railway runs the Union Canal, offering good towpath walks or boat rides and a museum to explain it all. Group boat rides can be booked at the Linlithgow Canal Centre (Manse Rd Basin, EH49 6AJ ☎ 01506 671215 ☝ lucs.org.uk).

HOUSE OF THE BINNS (Binns View, EH49 7NA ☎ 01786 812664 ☝ nts.org.uk) A little further away is this excellent merchant's house from the early 17th century. Set in beautifully landscaped parkland overlooking the River Forth, the building is surprisingly original, as was the most notable recent inhabitant, long-serving MP Tam Dalyell (d2017), firebrand left-winger in more than four decades in the UK Parliament. It is curious that he wasn't actually called Dalyell, but took his mother's name to become Sir Thomas Dalyell of the Binns, 11th Baronet and live in this glorious house.

PRESERVED RAILWAY Linlithgow is also the stop for the Bo'ness and Kinneil Railway (catch a bus from Linlithgow). See page 179.

Polmont (25 miles from Edinburgh) also had a branch line a couple of miles east of the station, going north to Bo'ness, but although this no longer runs as a through service, the branch – which was kept on for freight after passenger services stopped – has partly been revived as the rather wonderful heritage **BO'NESS AND KINNEIL RAILWAY** (page 179). Bo'ness, in case you wondered, stands for Borrowstouness, which no-one ever says or writes. Except here, just the once.

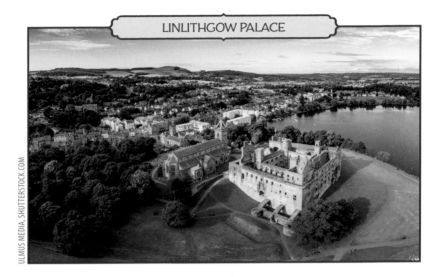

LINLITHGOW PALACE

ULMUS MEDIA, SHUTTERSTOCK.COM

The fine *Avon Viaduct* follows, over the river, taking us into West Lothian. The 442-yard 23-arch bridge was constructed in 1839–41 for the Edinburgh and Glasgow Railway.

Next stop is **Linlithgow**. The station building on the left (north) is a listed building, and is a surviving station of the original E&G Railway. The adjacent old station hotel, the Star and Garter, suffered a devastating fire in 2010, and I thought they'd perhaps pull the whole thing down. I'm delighted to say it's been well restored and offers good food. Not that the place is short of hostelries – next door in a bar called Platform 3, and further into town in a pub with the intriguing name, The Four Marys. They are not the ones you might guess – have a look at the front for an explanation. See box, page 44, for the town's other wonderful attractions.

Linlithgow station is also the location of the oldest railway photograph in the world, taken in 1845. It is, of course, fuzzy by later standards, but showed a bit of track, a shed and a view of part of the town. After a night out in the Star and Garter, you might be fuzzy by modern standards too!

Soon we will get grand views – again to the left (north) – of the entire broad Forth Valley, including the tidal Firth across to the mountains at the other side. But only glimpses between here and the end of the line.

Winchburgh Junction follows, unusually in a cutting, which allows trains to turn left (north) across the Forth Bridge without going into Edinburgh. We take the right fork.

Winchburgh Tunnel is followed by the *Bathgate Junction* trailing from the right, where that line (also from Glasgow) joins us. Views left include the tops of the various Forth Bridges, and Edinburgh Airport control tower. If you are eagle-eyed you can see Arthur's Seat and Edinburgh Castle ahead left, but certainly you can see the Pentland Hills south of Edinburgh ahead right.

Next is **Edinburgh Park** – a new station opened in 2003 which serves the eponymous business park and the Hermiston Gait shopping centre, and is a useful tram interchange getting you to the airport in about 10 minutes. It's about a mile from the South Gyle shopping centre, but that has its own station (also on the tram route) on the line from the Forth Bridge to Edinburgh, which we soon join at *Saughton Junction* (the so-far unelectrified lines of our left). Murrayfield rugby stadium follows on the left – the sight of so many dramas in the Six Nations championship – and then *we* run on to three junctions in quick succession (called *Haymarket West*, *Central* and *East*), which take us past a rail triangle on the right giving access to the Edinburgh Southside and Junction Line (which lets freight trains avoid the city centre stations, see comment on page 110). The Caledonian Main Line then joins from the south (this is today better known as part of the West Coast Main Line from Euston and Carlisle (page 32)).

Next we fly past *Haymarket depot* where you might see some of the famed HST InterCity 125 diesels, the ones with chisel-shaped ends, which

THE SHOCKINGLY NEW

For a country that today runs electric trains so well, Scotland's first foray into this form of power was rather hesitant and dangerous. The first electric line was a temporary one for the Edinburgh Industrial Exhibition of 1886. It had 2ft 6in gauge track and third rail power, and it was only a quarter-mile-long novelty ride. Afterwards, the owner of Carstairs House bought the train and built a 1½-mile-long line to take him from his home to the main-line station. As the *Leeds Times* reported in 1899:

Scotland has **SO MANY WATERFALLS** that it is not surprising to find a beginning made in utilising their power for electric railways. The residence of Mr. J. Monteith, Carstairs House, has recently been united to Carstairs Junction by an electric line

one and a quarter miles long, running through the grounds of the mansion. Messrs Anderson and Munro, of Glasgow, are the engineers of the line, which is worked by the Cleghorn Falls, some three miles distant on the River Mouse.

Mr Monteith, a fan of this new electric power he had installed throughout his house, was sadly electrocuted when he tripped over the railway and fell on the live rail. After that, the family used horses to pull the coach. But it was street tramways that first adopted electric traction in Scotland, usually with overhead wires. Eventually there were 21 tramways in Scotland running hundreds of miles, before they were driven out by the more flexible motor bus. But in the 21st century, trams have returned in Edinburgh.

are enjoying their senior years here pulling much lighter loads at less than their original 125mph. They echo the A4 steam locos of *Mallard* days which did just the same, and were also streamlined. So good was the refurb of these iconic HSTs when they came here that the review in *Rail* magazine was entitled 'The Next King of Scotland'. Then we head into busy **Haymarket** and through *Haymarket Tunnel* along Princes Street Gardens beneath the famous castle (high on the right – can you seriously imagine attacking up those cliffs?) and with Princes Street and the rocket-like Scott Monument high on the left (in front of the old Jenner's department store building) and through the *Mound Tunnel* into splendid **Edinburgh Waverley**. You have arrived in Scotland's most spectacular city! (More on this terminus and wonderful city on page xvi.)

OTHER EDINBURGH–GLASGOW ROUTES
SHOPPERS, STOPPERS & SHOCKERS

Rather surprisingly, perhaps, for outsiders, there are five rail routes between Edinburgh and Glasgow. All still running, all electrified. Indeed, this smacks of rival companies once trying to reach the same termini, but because the lines also served a thriving set of towns – in fact, often created them – they have survived, and thanks to Scotland's positive attitude to railways, UK government financing and the UK-wide infrastructure firm Network Rail's sterling (and indeed Stirling) efforts, they have been electrified and modernised. Apart from the Falkirk route (detailed previously), the four others are (not mentioning all the myriad small stations):

EDINBURGH TO GLASGOW VIA CUMBERNAULD*
1HR 17MINS, 49 MILES

This starts out along the same line as the above, but instead of stopping at Falkirk High goes to Falkirk Grahamston. In fact, it performs an odd pirouette with the above more direct line – it parts company with it shortly after leaving **Glasgow Queen Street**, crawls over *Sighthill West Jn* to reach **Springburn, Robroyston** (another welcome reopening – in fact it has reopened twice, exactly a century apart, in 1919 and 2019), where in town there is a monument to show where Scottish independence fighter William Wallace was captured by English troops in 1305 (as the film *Braveheart* portrayed, it ends shockingly badly for him), then **Stepps** (good for country walks into the Seven Lochs Wetland Park with splendid views on the right day – although there are days when any bit of Scotland would qualify as wetlands).

It then crosses the M80 Motorway into **Gartcosh** (7¾ miles), **Greenfaulds** (13¼ miles) and **Cumbernauld** (14 miles), where you can change for the **MOTHERWELL–CUMBERNAULD LINE.** (Cumbernauld was a pioneering new town after the war, nicknamed Noddytown by some Glaswegians who moved out there from the bomb-damaged slums because of its then futuristic buildings. But at least it had the rather sweet film *Gregory's Girl* made there.) We go under the other (Falkirk High) line, then a branch from that line joins before a major rail triangle on our left with the main line from Edinburgh to Perth, then after **Camelon** (mentioned because it is the closest stop to the Falkirk Wheel and the Kelpies, but not very close to either) and at **Falkirk Grahamston** (one benefit of having the two Falkirk stations is that this one can be served by expresses from London King's Cross to the Highlands) we rejoin the Falkirk High route to run into **Edinburgh**. There is talk of restoring a freight line to Grangemouth for passenger use, and being Scotland this might just happen. It takes off northeast after Falkirk Grahamston, but the line is hugely busy with freight, and faces only towards Glasgow, so how this would run is not clear.

GLASGOW–EDINBURGH VIA CARSTAIRS LINE*
1HR 20MINS, 56 MILES

The longest of the five routes. This simply uses the two arms of the Y-shaped West Coast Main Line from England. The terminus in Glasgow is therefore Glasgow Central. The only extra bit is the short connecting chord at Carstairs, the junction of the Y – a rather tight curve if you are taking a through train. Main stations served include (from **Glasgow Central**), **Cambuslang**, **Motherwell**, **Carstairs**, **Kirknewton**, **Curriehill**, **Wester Hailes** and **Kingsknowe** and **Slateford** (look out for an apparent railway viaduct to the right, or the south. It's an aqueduct and as remarked elsewhere, it's obvious why the canal builders could easily switch to railways. They were called railway navvies – navigators – for a reason!). Finally, it passes through **Edinburgh Haymarket** and ends at **Edinburgh Waverley**.

THE SHOTTS LINE*
1HR 10MINS (BUT CAN TAKE A LOT LONGER IF YOU CATCH THE STOPPER), 46 MILES

This uses the same route as the Carstairs Line at each end but cuts across through Shotts to shorten the journey and serve other places (although if it stops at all of them it will be a longish ride. A Scots comic once related how he was endlessly stopping at places he'd never heard of in his tedious Sunday ride – so get the faster service if you might feel the same!). Coming from **Glasgow Central**, it leaves the England-bound WCML after **Uddingston** at

THE CENTRAL BELT

1 The Fife Coastal Path between Kirkcaldy and Burntisland 2 Linlithgow Canal Centre 3 Falkirk Wheel 4 Callendar House, Falkirk 5 Aberdour is one of the region's prettiest stations, with the castle just adjacent 6 St Andrew's Kirk, North Berwick 7 Leaving North Queensferry

Uddingston Junction, then goes east through **Belshill, Holytown, Carfin, Cleland, Hartswood** and **Shotts**. This little town was once huge in coal mining and ironworking – as the fine statue of a metalworker in the centre suggests. Next comes **Fauldhouse, Breich** (which, according to one recent survey, was the second least-used station in Scotland, yet has somehow bagged itself a new station, electrification and modern trains!), **Addiewell** and **West Calder**. Soon afterwards we join the Edinburgh-bound arm of the WCML at *Midcalder Junction* just before **Kirknewton**. After **Edinburgh Waverley**, some trains continue to **North Berwick** or **Dunbar**, a useful cross-country link.

THE NORTH CLYDE & BATHGATE LINE*
1HR 10MINS, 44 MILES

This starts with the busy North Clyde route west of Glasgow from **Helensburgh** and **Balloch** through **Glasgow Queen Street** (Low Level), out through various eastern suburban stations including the hopefully named **Coatbridge Sunnyside** (I've never been through there when it was not grey or raining!) to **Airdrie, Caldercruix** and **Bathgate**, and thanks to a brilliant recent electrification and reopening, on to **Edinburgh Park, Edinburgh Haymarket** and **Edinburgh Waverley**. Favourite station name: Caldercruix. It is thought the name might derive from crooks in the River Calder. Crooks meaning bends, not thieving wee bampots!

THE CATHCART CIRCLE*
GLASGOW CENTRAL TO GLASGOW CENTRAL
26MINS, 7 MILES

In Glasgow's inner southern suburbs there is a curious little 5½-mile-long circular route that takes about half an hour to scoot round. **THE CATHCART CIRCLE** line leaps over the river, dips its toe in the Southside of Glasgow and scoots back to Central. But it turned out that it quite liked the other side of the Clyde, for there were soon branches running off it to Newton and Neilston. So the route's shape, which had been like a full sack held by the neck, now remains the sack but with two legs on it too.

Luckily the electric trains go both ways, otherwise their wheels would wear down on one side more than the other – so people halfway along can judge whether to best go clockwise or anticlockwise to get to the city centre. The destination of Cathcart Circle trains is always Glasgow Central, but would be a bit embarrassing to announce that at Glasgow Central so they pretend they are going somewhere else en route and then quickly sneak back acting as if they are a completely new service, as if to say – 'what? nothing odd about me!'

The builders of the line in the 1880s and '90s seemed to be doing something daft – building stations where only cows or sheep lived – but they cannily realised, as with the 'Metroland' near London – that if you build the line, the houses will follow, and to pay for those houses, the people in them will need to go to work. On trains.

Soon housing gathered around the ten stations, and at its peak there were 45 trains a day in each direction round the circle – all done by steam engines. Today it's about half that.

The Cathcart Circle entered the social fabric of the city and folklore, too. There was even a novel set on it, *Snooker Tam of the Cathcart Railway* (1919). It says:

'It is the most convenient line, and the cheapest thing out of LIPTON'S [grocers].'

And goes on to suggest some romantic possibilities:

'Indeed, many a lover has found it is better to invest fourpence in the CATHCART CIRCLE than two shillings at the picture-house [where canoodling in the back row was not unknown as you stayed for as many repeats of the film as you wished]. It is a DEADLY TRAP of bachelors, and the hope of pretty typists.

All single men arriving in "Glasca" are advised to look for lodgings around the CIRCLE. No wonder – at the five-thirty can be seen everything from a GEISHA to a MADONNA. The Venus from Pollokshields runs shoulders with the Gaby from Cathcart.'

Well it was supposed to be comic at the time, but you'd be hard put to find a typist nowadays, and daren't even *think* whether she was pretty or not, let alone wonder whether a trip on the Cathcart Circle, rather than, say, the Orient Express, would today be considered romantic enough for a kiss and a cuddle. But people don't change that much – one of the daily papers has a column entitled 'Rush Hour Crush' where people try to make contact with others who caught their eye on the daily commute.

Back to the railway! The stations were originally – and still are in some cases – mostly rather attractive island platforms with a single building bearing an enormous coolie hat-type roof, held up by ornamental wooden brackets. These huge overhangs had the benefit of sheltering a large number of people from the Glaswegian rain (probably not that romantic). And in the snow with those chalet-like roofs, they can look positively Alpine.

THE ROUTE DESCRIBED

Leaving **Glasgow Central**, the clockwise trains (which run like clockwork, obviously) arrive at **Pollokshields East**, at which platforms you can see the route where you will return in half an hour above right. Signs saying 'Alight

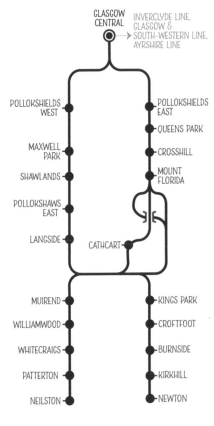

GLASGOW CENTRAL
INVERCLYDE LINE, GLASGOW & SOUTH-WESTERN LINE, AYRSHIRE LINE

POLLOKSHIELDS WEST
POLLOKSHIELDS EAST
QUEENS PARK
MAXWELL PARK
CROSSHILL
SHAWLANDS
MOUNT FLORIDA
POLLOKSHAWS EAST
LANGSIDE
CATHCART
MUIREND
KINGS PARK
WILLIAMWOOD
CROFTFOOT
WHITECRAIGS
BURNSIDE
PATTERTON
KIRKHILL
NEILSTON
NEWTON

for the Tramway' must confuse some visitors – there are no trams (like having a shopping centre signposted Centre Court near Wimbledon. Very clever – unless you are Japanese with little English!). It's a huge hangar-like arts space, a bit like the Tate Modern in London in size, home to dance, visual arts and exhibitions. Hereabouts our line dives and then rises to weave through the complexities of other railways and streets.

Next comes **Queens Park** (original station building). The park (200 yards south of the station), which gave its name to Queen's Park Football Club, is named not, as often said, after Victoria but after tragic Mary, Queen of Scots who lost a battle hereabouts, after which things famously got worse. Also going downhill fast are the general populace, when it's been snowing. It's a favourite spot for sledging!

After **Crosshill** (the name probably meant Gorse Hill originally) comes **Mount Florida**: alight here for Hampden Park, or continue on to **Cathcart** (original station building, and advertises on its name board that it's a short stroll from Holmwood, a villa in the care of the National Trust for Scotland at 61 Netherlee Road, where you can see the richly embellished architecture of Alexander 'Greek' Thomson).

Heading back towards Glasgow Central, you'll come to **Langside** (spacious, good views towards Cathkin Braes), and **Pollokshaws East**, which is on a bridge with the White Cart Water flowing underneath. This makes a prettier sight in the huge Pollok Country Park, which is only a few hundred yards' stroll west and contains another National Trust property, the stately home of Pollok House (see box, page 34), containing a superb collection of Spanish art and, they tell us, 'vast servants' quarters'. (Why they wanted vast servants I don't know, they must have cost a bit to feed, but it's cleverly marketed as 'Scotland's answer to *Downton Abbey*', so maybe they were shaped like Mrs Patmore in that TV series.) The park also contains the world-famous Burrell

SCOTLAND'S LUNACY LINE

An unusual railway was that built by the Edinburgh District Lunacy Board and opened in 1905, running from the Bathgate branch to Bangour where a large asylum was built. The local MP for Linlithgowshire objected, arguing that the lunacy board was itself going a bit crackers in running a railway (and also a water-supply company). In fact, it was not unusual for such large psychiatric hospitals to have their own railways to bring in coal, food, patients and staff, and this hospital was a good, progressive one built on 'village'

lines. Come World War I, it was taken over for the war wounded, who arrived in ambulance trains from Southampton Docks. The odd little 1½-mile-long railway – which the public could use, too – was closed in 1921.

In June 2020, revellers held an illegal rave in the derelict hospital, despite national Covid lockdown restrictions, and consequently smashed up all the windows, destroyed the hospital's own chapel and set fire to the place. Some people might think that was a different kind of lunacy.

Collection (see box, page 34) or at least should do. Next is **Shawlands**, after which we very soon cross over the **KILMARNOCK LINE** (which has its own station, Pollokshaws West, right by that park). Finally, we reach **Maxwell Park** (really well restored, in fact faithfully reconstructed, station building), and **Pollokshields West**. This couldn't be more on a contrast with the east variety of the same name, with its inner city-feel, as here it is spacious villas, genteel suburbia, tennis courts and bowling clubs.

Football traffic could be intense on this line with several grounds nearby (one international against the 'auld enemy' – England – at nearby Hampden Park required 20 specials from Central in the 1950s, with about a dozen more special trains from outside Glasgow at stations to the south). On the last stretch of the Circle, look out to the right and you'll see Pollokshields East next to and a little below us, where we were a few minutes ago!

Two other branches spin off this circular route. The **NEILSTON BRANCH** heads southwest off at **Cathcart** (going clockwise) to **Muirend**, **Williamwood**, **Whitecraigs** (great views follow in good weather), **Patterton** and **Neilston**. The **NEWTON BRANCH** takes off to the east either from **Mount Florida** (clockwise trains) or **Langside** (anticlockwise) and goes to **Kings Park**, **Croftfoot**, **Burnside**, **Kirkhill** and **Newton**.

I can't say whether having four stations called Pollok-something causes a few people to get their Polloks in a twist. Possibly not as disastrously as the tipsy American businessman who rushed on to his plane home to Oakland, California, as the doors were about to close. Only to find after take-off it was going to *Auckland*, New Zealand – a 14-hour trip!

THE FIFE CIRCLE**
EDINBURGH WAVERLEY TO EDINBURGH WAVERLEY
2HRS 10MINS, 60 MILES

The **FIFE CIRCLE** is a very useful route around some southern towns of that county, diverging just north of the Forth Bridge to the west, looping through those places and rejoining the main Edinburgh–Dundee line, making – as it says on the tin! – a round route. Well, OK, a balloon shape. If you are in Edinburgh and fancy a trip over the Forth Bridge (twice), this is ideal.

The really good news – well done Scotland, again! – is that it is going to be enhanced by one pretty certain extension during the lifetime of this

book, may well enjoy another one, and a third – less likely but possible – is being mooted.

The extension that will happen soonest is from Thornton Junction east to Leven, possibly with a station at Cameron Bridge. The track is mostly all there, already owned by Network Rail, so how hard can it be? But stations need to be built. The second and most interesting extension is from the west, taking the recently reopened and electrified line from Stirling to Alloa, and using existing freight-only tracks, reaching Dunfermline on the Fife Circle and making a very useful west–east route. This is quite possible, given political will, which Scotland seems to have.

The third extension is in St Andrews in the north of the county. The town lost its link to Leuchars, the junction on the main line not part of the Fife Circle, in 1969. It was a stupid cut, as thousands of students at the famous university there – including presumed future queen, Kate Middleton – had to decamp into buses and taxis, along with golfers and tourists. The town simply can't handle all that road traffic, although I think it fair to say lovely St Andrews doesn't need a shot in the arm economically as with the other two, if that were the motivation. But it would cope with the town's success better. Why not meet demand as well as create it? The track and stations have long gone, so it would be a major piece of work, but worth doing.

So what did the railways do before the sensational Forth Bridge was built? The answer is quite surprising… see box, page 58.

THE ROUTE DESCRIBED

The current line is as follows: if coming from Edinburgh (Waverley or Haymarket), you pass through **South Gyle**, **Edinburgh Gateway** and **Dalmeny**. While on the *Forth Bridge* (see box, page 72), keep an eye out for Rosyth Docks (on the north bank to the left, west, of our bridge). After **North Queensferry** (note the brilliant mosaic on the left) and two tunnels, **Inverkeithing** sits at a junction on the East Coast Main Line. If going clockwise round the Fife Circle, we branch left (or rather, straight-on-ish) and turn west for **Rosyth**, an important shipyard even today, where ships such as our new aircraft carriers were built, the biggest vessels yet for the Royal Navy (which is why the Forth Bridges needed to be so high) and frigates turned out for… erm… frigatting!

Soon a freight line trails in from the left (west), which could be important because this route could soon form a new passenger line from Alloa. Then comes **Dunfermline Town** and **Dunfermline Queen Margaret**, before we head under the M90 Motorway and north and east to **Cowdenbeath**, **Lochgelly**, **Cardenden** and the lovely rolling hills of Fife, which belie the struggle men once had to hew energy in the form of coal out of the ground below – as the freight lines still here and there suggest. Now men hew energy out of thin air with the giant wind turbines around Fife. Fewer jobs, no doubt, but fewer mining illnesses and deaths and a whole lot less pollution for the same electricity to be generated. **Glenrothes with Thornton** comes next, just before we rejoin the main line at *Thornton South Junction*.

The main line goes back to Edinburgh via the sizable town of **Kirkcaldy** (hikers note: the Fife Coastal Path links up this and stations south), **Kinghorn**, followed by *Kinghorn Tunnel* (265yds, curved), **Burntisland** (the railway swerves off from what used to be a terminus for a ferry to Granton, see page 59), **Aberdour** (what a pretty station, with the castle and gardens adjacent)

Edinburgh as far as Kirkcaldy also features in the
EAST COAST MAIN LINE to Aberdeen (page 67).

and **Dalgety Bay**. It rejoins our outward route before Inverkeithing, heading south for the Forth Bridge (by the way, if you look right on the approach you get a very interesting lengthways view of the two Forth road bridges), and thus back to Edinburgh Haymarket and Edinburgh Waverley.

SEASIDE EXCURSIONS
TWO GREAT DAYS OUT FROM SCOTLAND'S TWO BIG CITIES

TO WEMYSS BAY**
BONNIE & CLYDE
1HR, 30 MILES

Glasgow has a great network of suburban lines, some pretty and some, frankly, not. Paisley Canal, one of the termini, is not exactly Paisley patterned (but a

THE FIRST OF FORTH – & FIRST IN THE WORLD!

In the 1840s and '50s, bridge builders had neither the skills nor the technology – nor the money – to fling a bridge high across a deep, storm-tossed estuary like the Firth of Forth. But they were desperate to provide services north from Edinburgh (and England) to Dundee and Aberdeen, and to do so, crucially, without using the lines of rival companies to the west.

The answer suggested, eccentric though it seems, was to run trains off the end of piers. That they didn't sink was thanks to a 'floating railway', as they called it. What we would today call a train ferry – a roll-on, roll-off service, the first of its sort. It ran from Burntisland in Fife to Leith on the Edinburgh shore. Very few people know of this now – yet it had a profound effect on world transport.

To make it possible the engineer in question – Thomas Bouch (you might have heard of him in connection with the Tay Bridge, but he was not yet disgraced by that disaster) – designed and built the first link span, the tilting ramp that allows all today's ferries to roll traffic, road

or rail, off a ship at any state of tide and land them on terra firma. It pioneered the concept of train ferries – that is, ships with rails let into their decks or holds – such as the link between the North and South Islands in New Zealand, or mainland Italy and Sicily.

The problem wasn't really the passengers. They are self-propelled, usually, and can get on and off boats as needed, climbing gangplanks and ladders. It was freight loads – particularly heavy ones like stone, loose ones like flour, messy ones like coal, fragile ones like bottles – these are not self-propelled and very slow and tedious to transfer into a boat and back on to another train.

This generally totally forgotten pioneering Scottish service influenced later more famous counterparts such as those between London and Paris. The day express *The Golden Arrow* let passengers climb aboard a fast ferry at Folkestone. The train stayed in England. But the *Night Ferry* – and lots of freight wagons – rolled up ramps into the hold of a ship at Dover. Bit of a BONG-BONG as you went aboard over the steepish

welcome reopening in 1990). One that I loved is the hour-long trip to **Wemyss Bay** (pronounced 'Weems Bay') from **Glasgow Central**.

Central station is by far the better of the city's termini, and the interior is spacious with many fascinating details, such as the splendid covered carriageway on the street, the elliptical wooden buildings inside the concourse and, on your left looking towards the trains, the 'CR' initials carved above a passageway – standing for Caledonian Railway. In 2023, exactly 100 years out of date!

The station is always busy, with trains to many parts of England as well as south-of-the-Clyde Scotland. Clearly the Caledonian expected the Sassenach trains to arrive in a great hurry, judging by the massive buffer stops.

I said south of the Clyde, but we're not to start with. We leap quickly across the Clyde and rapidly diverge right. There are all sorts of junctions for the suburban lines you can see on the route map in the carriages, and we whizz

SUPERSTOCK

ramp supposedly sleeping in your berth, I seem to recall. Car-ferry operators took even longer to realise roll-on, roll-off was better than craning the cars aboard one-by-one, which I can just recall still happening about 1960.

Mind you, the first ferry on the Forth (and in the world, using the specially built *Leviathan*), which began on 3 February 1850, involved even steeper angles on the track, which long train carriages or locomotives might not have managed, but it was good enough for the short four-wheeled wagons of the day, hauled aboard by cables. Fast passenger paddle-steamers also left from Granton with trains waiting to speed passengers north at Burntisland.

The 'floating railway' was a big success, with a number of ships operating day and night. It was put out of business eventually by the Forth Bridge a few miles west of its route (although the fast passenger boats carried on for many decades and there are moves to restore them now). And that bridge wasn't built, as first planned, to Sir Thomas Bouch's design, because of the catastrophic failure of his bridge over the Tay, next firth north (see box, page 69). But not only did the now-derided Bouch build many good bridges that lasted (and very affordably to startling designs), but, you now know, he also invented the roll-on, roll-off ferries we all use.

Wemyss Bay station (KENNY LAM, VISITSCOTLAND)

61

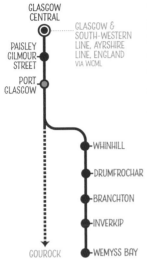

through some uninspiring suburbs. Never fear, it gets a lot better. After a stop at **Paisley Gilmour Street** (near the airport on our right, probably getting its own branch) we swing right, back towards the Clyde. After **Port Glasgow** there are bonnie views of the Clyde Estuary, with its massive shipping-lane markers making clear its importance, past and present.

Soon we are diverging left on our own ten-mile-long branch (the mileposts are on the right if you like that sort of thing). A currently closed station called IBM (because of the factory) and **Inverkip** follow and then we reach **Wemyss Bay**, the most perfectly preserved Edwardian station in Scotland. Take a while to walk around the concourse near the booking office and appreciate the glazing that floods this cheerful place with light, unlike so many gloomy stations of that era. Also check out the great station bookshop.

A ramp leads down to the waiting Caledonian MacBrayne steamer to Rothesay on the beautiful island of Bute. I'd take a boat there and back myself, as there isn't a lot to do in Wemyss Bay. But if not doing a lot is what suits you, you can take a walk along the beach to look at the views, perhaps paddling across the stream (to the left looking seawards), or crossing it on the bridge, in which case you have crossed into Ayrshire (and you can give yourself Ayrs) and entered the village of Skelmorlie.

If you're feeling lazy, sit in the Sea View Café across the road and enjoy a snack – they have some great salads and cakes. Here you can watch the splendid clock tower of the 1903 station, and marvel at how the ferry manages to come in just before your return train departs. On returning to the station, notice what's carved above one of the windows: *CR*.

NORTH BERWICK[*]
FOR QUALITY STREET... & BLACK MAGIC
30MINS, 22 MILES

A day out to **North Berwick** from Edinburgh is fun and quick, being less than 30 miles along the coast to the east. It is connected by a fast, clean, reliable, direct train (33 minutes) which takes a four-mile branch off the East Coast Main Line on its way to the other better-known Berwick. It goes from Haymarket or Waverley stations. Here's a brief guide.

Someone once ludicrously titled North Berwick 'the Biarritz of the North'. One wonders if they had seen either of them. But it's guaranteed to be

worthwhile on any half-decent day because of the superb location – wide clean sandy beaches, rock pooling or scrambling around rocks, plentiful seabirds – and the best view you can imagine.

The less-than-grand railway station is on the edge of town, the engineers having understandably decided not to try to reach the much lower level of the town but stay up on the coastal plain. The branch line opened in 1850 and transformed North Berwick's economy, but the feebleness of early steam engines meant that the service to here from **Drem** on the main line was for a while one horse-drawn carriage.

Go left out of the station and then right (noticing St Baldred's squat church opposite, and there's a Blackadder Church elsewhere in the town) down Station Hill. Carry on down Beach Road to the beach. We go left down Victoria Road to the far side of the little harbour which includes pretty fishermen's cottages and a lifeboat station.

At the end, notice the touching memorial to Glaswegian student Kate Watson, who aged 19 gave her life here to save a drowning child in East Bay in 1889. The boy was saved and though she died, here she is immortalised rather beautifully.

Just beyond are the ruins and remains of St Andrew's Kirk, a scene of the most gruesome witchcraft four centuries ago – if the stories extracted under torture are to be believed. It was the story behind Shakespeare's *Macbeth*. It is an extraordinary tale, and you'll not find better evidence of witches anywhere.

On a somewhat sunnier subject, here is a great view of Berwick Law, the conical hill right behind the town (and note the thin arch on the top) and Bass Rock, another volcanic plug a mile or two out at sea.

Now Bass Rock – despite its having been once a prison, let's not call it the Alcatraz of the East – is home to thousands of screaming gannets. You can go out on a boat for a look at this and the dramatic coast nearby in summer months. It also has a strange natural tunnel going right through it, visible at low tide.

But you can get a close-up by other means. Down by the shore is an ornithologist's dream, the Scottish Seabird Centre, which by means of live television cameras gives you close-ups of gannets doing whatever they do, as well as puffins, which look like silly toy birds made up for paperback book covers but which turn out to be something like seagoing rabbits in their behaviour – burrowing holes to live in, etc. Wonder if they're any good in a pie?

TANTALLON CASTLE & BASS ROCK

KENNY LAM, VISITSCOTLAND

This promontory was once linked to the town by a bridge at high tide, and the chapel was important for medieval pilgrims making their way across from here to St Andrews in Fife. Going back up Victoria Street away from the sea, you will find in Quality Street (straight ahead) plenty of places to eat plaices and other food, as well as tourist information and toilets up the far end.

Why Quality Street? Are the people toffee-nosed? (For North American readers, it is a brand of British sweets – candies – once much loved by Saddam Hussein of all people, but if we are on a box-of-chocolates theme North Berwick is much more like Black Magic with its witchy history.)

Actually toffee-nosed is exactly it. The people who once lived here thought themselves above the average, hence the name.

Go right at the top of Quality Street and pass the subsequent St Andrew's Church (also ruined) and then left up Law Road towards Law School at the very top.

We are heading for the 613ft hill itself which is so dramatically and apparently artificially emerging from the plain that it looks as if it could be a spoil heap for a mine. But this is no slag, it's a crag – crag and tail, or a volcanic plug left when the landscape was scoured out by glaciers, as is Edinburgh Castle rock and many more round here. The path towards the Law is a rough road to the left, through a stile and around the hill's right flank. Soon the path to the top goes off left. I'd advise sticking to the paths as much as you can because otherwise you may find yourself clambering over dangerously steep wet rocks and damaging fragile hillside too. I wouldn't take tearaway toddlers and wheelchairs are quite out of the question. It's all at your own risk.

But it is absolutely worth it for one of the greatest views in Britain on a fine day, and I don't exaggerate. At the top you can look back south inland over Traprain Law six miles away, another crag and tail formation where the Romans encountered a tribal settlement. Beyond are the lovely Lammermuir Hills, combed towards the southwest by great glaciers. Slightly to the right are the Pentland Hills and Arthur's Seat in Edinburgh.

Back towards the sea we have a bird's-eye view of the town and Bass Rock seems close enough to touch. On the coast facing it is the romantic ruin of tantalising Tantallon Castle, easily visited if you are carborne.

Further out there are flat islands such as Fidra, formed by the liquid rock of magma intruding in horizontal shelves into whatever landscape there then was. Beyond them is the Kingdom of Fife and beyond that, if it is very clear, I'm told you can see the Grampian Mountains of the real Highlands.

And to the east (if you are reading this on the train or in an armchair rather than on the hilltop, where it will be rather obvious), the North Sea stretches to the wide horizon.

The thin arch we saw from the town turns out to be made out of a whale's jawbone. Whaling was once a vital industry locally, and the first whale jawbone was landed in North Berwick in 1709, although the monument has been replaced over the years.

Not surprisingly this excellent vantage point, easily seen from Edinburgh's Calton Hill, has been used in conflicts over the centuries, from a medieval flaming beacon to a tower to warn of Napoleonic invasion (the unlikelihood of his coming by this route didn't seem to have stopped the Scots joining in the national anti-French hysteria) and a World War II bunker which probably did have something to look at as Nazi bombers lined up for their run west to attack Rosyth. The remains of both eras are obvious here at the top.

If you are returning to the station, you can save your weary feet a hill descent and climb by going left at the crossroads at the beginning of the hill down to town and following Clifford Road round on the level to the station.

Crossing the Tay Rail Bridge at Dundee
(BRUCE GALLOWAY)

FIRTH TO LAST

Edinburgh TO Aberdeen

2½HRS, 129 MILES****

This ride (a continuation of the East Coast Main Line) is scenically, geographically and, in engineering terms, one of the best – you will not be bored for a second. The monstrous, magnificent and breathtaking Forth Bridge is only one of many treats. The Tay Bridge, too, where – as the photo opposite clearly shows – the piers of the original bridge bore witness to a terrible event.

EDINBURGH TO DUNDEE***
BRIDGES TO ADVENTURE
1HR 10MINS, 59 MILES

Starting off, we pass through an echoing canyon between Edinburgh Castle, high up to our left, and Princes Street to our right, through a tunnel to **Haymarket** station in the city's West End – a short distance that you could easily walk. Even odder, then, to recall that there once were two more stations in between (called Princes Street and Exhibition) plus another on a rival route nearby – all part of the expensive duplication of stations and routes by rival companies before grouping in 1923 and nationalisation in 1948. The huge stadium on the right just after Haymarket is Murrayfield, home to Scottish rugby.

Soon after the line to Glasgow diverges left, we go through **South Gyle** station, then **Edinburgh Gateway**, which connects with trams serving Edinburgh Airport. Now you can see the mileposts counting up from zero again – at the 8½ milepost, there is an exciting glimpse looking ahead and a little to the right

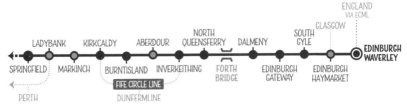

(on the starboard bow, as a sailor on the train would put it) of the looming **Forth Bridge*****. As we near the bridge, a line from Linlithgow joins from the left (just after we go under a main road) and then we reach **Dalmeny***** station. If you'd like to look at the fantastic Forth bridges from ground level, and have a poke around the fascinating town of South Queensferry, way down below on the shoreline, then Dalmeny would be the port of call by a local train. For the story of the Forth Bridge – one of the seven wonders of the world in engineering – see the box on page 72, but for the moment sit back and enjoy the astonishing views as you soar like an aircraft high over the roofs to South Queensferry and out above the waters of the Forth.

On the left is the Forth Road Bridge, a far lighter suspension design compared with the staggeringly massive, cantilevered monster we are crossing and behind it the new Queensferry Crossing bridge. All are built to be able to clear full-sized ships heading up to the busy docks at the head of the Forth (west, to your left) and any warships heading for Rosyth Dockyards (on the far shore). On the right are islands, some fortified from various wars (such as Inch Garvie, just below on the right), some with holy relics.

The last time I crossed this wonderful bridge, an autumnal sun was setting to the west, turning the Forth into a blazing cauldron of red and yellow, merging in the sky into apricots, blues and purples. Looking east into the inky blackness of the North Sea, a near full moon was rising, leaving a shimmering silver trail across the still, dark waters. Magic!

We hit **North Queensferry** – the name reminds us what was here before the bridges, and in fact lasted on another century after the rail bridge arrived – and get a view of Rosyth Dockyards to our left. **Inverkeithing** station is followed by a junction where we veer right and one side of the **FIFE CIRCLE LINE** (page 56) goes left. Following **Dalgety Bay**, look out after **Aberdour** station for the ruins of a castle on the right. There are excellent views across to Edinburgh here and sharply backwards, towards the Forth Bridge. You have to be this far away to appreciate its size.

Burntisland station is near oil-rig support yards: here I once spotted a fat seal close to the shore, swimming on his back and looking curiously up at the train. After **Kinghorn** and **Kirkcaldy** (see page 57 for more), the line swings north, across old coalfields and into the fertile farmland of the 'Kingdom of Fife', a land cut off on three sides

THE TAY BRIDGE DISASTER, THE 'DIVER' & BIRD POO

The Tay Bridge may not look as dramatic as the Forth Bridge, but it attracts different kinds of superlatives: the worst disaster, when the first bridge fell down on 28 December 1879; the longest rail bridge in Britain, at 2¼ miles; and the worst poem about a disaster ever written (by William Topaz McGonagall, who had just written two poems praising the strength of the bridge), which starts:

Beautiful railway bridge of
the silv'ry Tay
ALAS! I am very sorry to say
That ninety lives have
been taken away

It was the high girder section of the single-track bridge that blew down, taking a train and all 75 people on board to their doom. The fact that part of the bridge was gone was only ascertained by a worried railwayman crawling along the structure in the gale and darkness when he reached the gap (pictured).

Designer Thomas Bouch had not allowed enough strength for the wind pressure of gales, or indeed any allowance for wind. The cast-iron pillars and connecting work were badly made, patched up to look passable when they should have been rejected. The bridge was then poorly maintained; signs of deterioration were ignored. And as if that weren't a recipe for disaster, speed limits were also exceeded (even today, it's a long trundle).

Sir Thomas Bouch – he had just been knighted for his design! – lost a son-in-law in the disaster. Work had just started on his design

for a Forth Bridge; this was rapidly scrapped and redesigned. The Tay Bridge was rebuilt to a far better design, but you can see the piers of the old one sticking above the water alongside. Bouch died in disgrace soon afterwards.

Surprisingly, after the central high girders were lifted from the riverbed and the train found within, the repaired locomotive was run until 1919. And perhaps unsurprisingly, many railwaymen refused to drive the engine, nicknamed the *Diver*, over the new Tay Bridge which opened in 1887.

In 2003, when the current bridge was thoroughly refurbished and strengthened, 1,000 tonnes of bird droppings were scraped off! Grotty job. Now it's tip-top.

by sea and still very much its own place. (By the way, if foreigners find Firth of Forth a mouthful, they should try giving a football result

THE RIVETING YARN OF THE FORTH BRIDGE

The Forth Bridge, the railway bridge that opened in 1890, is an internationally recognised outline like that of the Taj Mahal or Statue of Liberty. Crossing it, you fly like a plane high over the rooftops of South Queensferry on the Edinburgh side, and the train – running 150ft above high water to allow shipping through – is completely dwarfed by the mighty structure.

It is far more massive than it needed to be because, not long before it was built, a trainload of passengers had disappeared under the waves when the Tay Bridge, on the next great inlet up the coast, had collapsed (see box, page 69). The same designer was about to build the Forth Bridge, so that project was swiftly shelved and thousands of tons of perhaps unnecessary steel were used to make it as strong as possible. It was also one of the first large bridges made of steel – as opposed to iron – so it was experimental in its tube and lattice construction.

It is 1½ miles long, the towers are 360ft tall and 55,000 tons of steel and 8 million rivets were used to build it.

'Painting the Forth Bridge' (all 145 acres of steelwork on the 1½-mile-long structure) became an international phrase for something you could never finish, because when you got to the end you had to start again to stop it rusting. When the cocked-up reprivatisation of the railways took place in 1996, they stopped painting it, and guess what – it started rusting, and had to be rescued at great expense. All is well again now, however.

Anyway, back to the spooky stuff – when the Forth Bridge was being built in 1890, the enormous cantilevered arms were reaching out to meet each other, but they were so huge that they couldn't exactly meet.

Although perfectly made and aligned, they were so big that the effect of the sun on the eastern side in the morning, and the west in the afternoon, could bend the structure enough to prevent perfect alignment. The solution was to send men inside the massive tubes, each itself large enough to take a London Tube train, to light bonfires and 'trick' the bridge, as it were, into thinking that it was sunny on both sides. The ends aligned perfectly, the bolts were dropped in and the last plates riveted up. But did all the men get out of the smoke-filled tubes? Is that knocking and groaning you can hear just the bridge expanding or the ghosts of something else?

That much may be pure myth. What is true though is the staggering toll of workers who died building the thing, in accidents or blown off while walking the high girders: 71 deaths by the best count (see the memorial at South Queensferry).

Even more recently I have heard a local widow talk of how a man died when he tripped on the highest part, probably because he would

such as East Fife five, Forfar four.) A supposed Edinburgh saying is: 'It tak's a lang spune to sup with a Fifer'. This may say something about Fifers' character, or just be a practical reality if you're trying to sup with them from Edinburgh!

After a junction where the **FIFE CIRCLE** route rejoins, we whistle through **Markinch, Ladybank** (where the **TAY COAST LINE** to Perth takes off left),

BUILDING THE COLOSSUS

SUPERSTOCK

We are now in full view of the Forth Bridge – that **STUPENDOUS** undertaking which is, by universal consent, held to be the **GREATEST ENGINEERING TRIUMPH** of the kind that has ever been consummated.
From a 1904 traveller's guide

keep his hands in his pockets against the cold and therefore couldn't save himself. It makes you realise when the Health and Safety mob festoon places like this with fussy walkways and handrails, they may have a point.

The bridge features in Hitchcock's great film, *The 39 Steps*, in an Iain Banks novel *The Bridge*, on some pound coins in your pocket and in the computer game 'Grand Theft Auto: San Andreas'. It's very well worth a walk round South Queensferry at the south end of the bridges, getting off at Dalmeny station. Spectacular.

And some wonderful news: soon the public should be able to ascend the North Queensferry tower by lift and also walk across the bridge from the south at a high level, thanks to a new visitor centre being built by Network Rail. I've seen the pictures and it will be breathtakingly brilliant; see 🖱 forthbridgeexperience.com.

Springfield* (the tall monument on top of a hill to the left is to Sir John Hope, Earl of Hopetoun, who by turning the fortunes of the Pensinsular War in 1808 indeed gave Britain hope. He also has a similar monument further down this line past Edinburgh at Haddington in East Lothian – both are inscribed 'by his affectionate and grateful tenantry' – and a statue in St Andrew Square, Edinburgh), **Cupar** and then **Leuchars***. This is the station

EDINBURGH TO ABERDEEN

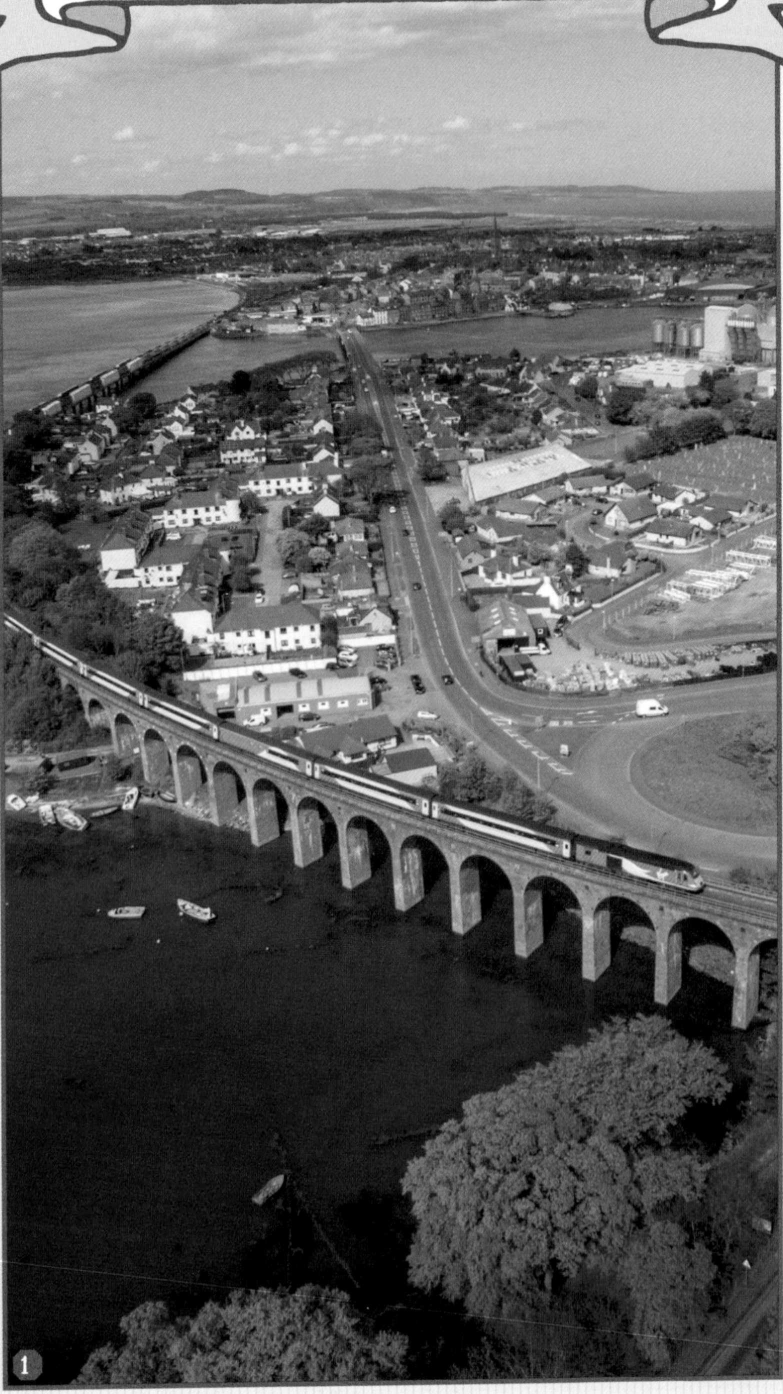

BRUCE GALLOWAY

1

1 Crossing the Ferryden Viaduct over the Montrose Basin
2 The V&A Museum of Design and RRS *Discovery* at Dundee's Waterfront redevelopment 3 The famous
Arbroath Smokie 4 Old Links Course, St Andrews 5 The City of Granite: Aberdeen

KENNY LAM, VISITSCOTLAND

S_KARAU, SHUTTERSTOCK.COM

for St Andrews (on the North Sea coast a couple of miles east), the ancient university town, spiritual home of world golf, and place of pilgrimage for the sport's followers. It used to have its own branch line connecting here. If you don't see some wealthy golfers getting off the train with all their kit, being helped into plush minibuses to go to their swanky hotels, sell your shares; there must be a global recession. Or maybe buy them, they will be cheap.

It's also the station for RAF Leuchars air base, which spent much of the Cold War batting probing Russians back across the North Sea (although now it's largely an army base), and for Scotland's oldest university which famously produced Prince William as a graduate in 2005.

By the way, I recall being here back in the land of semaphore signals (those waggling arms and manual signalboxes). South of Waverley, we had a 21st-century electrified railway with electronic computerised control; here we were in the 19th century, the lines little different from when they carried steam trains. Did anyone mind? No. Was it less safe? Certainly not. Was it less reliable? Nope. And they worked in a power cut!

On the very wiggly short run between here and the *Tay Bridge****, you glimpse distant views, sharply ahead on the right, then left as the train swings, of the city of Dundee, across the Firth of Tay.

Again, this firth offers great views. On the peaceful shore you may see a heron patiently stalking fish. To the west you can see the beautiful wide firth stretching up towards Perth; to the east the narrower entrance from the North Sea, and ahead, the city of Dundee. To the immediate right, down below are the stubs of the piers of the ill-fated first Tay Bridge (see box, page 69). If you can't see them from up on the train, look back as we curve off the bridge down into Dundee.

At just over two miles, the Tay Bridge is Britain's longest railway bridge, so you've plenty of time to contemplate the view. The hill behind Dundee city centre is Dundee Law and a now-closed branch line round behind there had a station by the prosaic name Back of Law.

DUNDEE TO ABERDEEN**
LOCH, DOCK & A SMOKING BARREL
1HR 10MINS, 71 MILES

As we descend off the bridge and curve on to the shore, we join the **TAY COAST LINE** running along the river's north bank from Perth, and soon we arrive at **Dundee** station, somewhat sunk into the city. Known for jute, jam and journalism, Dundee has never been the prettiest Scottish city but has cleaned up its act and made much of its university (once part of St Andrews) and its links with great explorers. The hinterland of Angus, behind the city, is as fertile and attractive as Fife. My favourite products of Dundee are *The Beano* (a comic), William McGonagall, the world's worst poet, and yummy Dundee cake. And don't miss the startling V&A Museum on the waterside.

After tunnelling under the town, we emerge by the docks and run through the increasingly attractive seaside settlements of **Broughty Ferry**, **Balmossie**, **Monifieth**, **Barry Links** (24 passengers in the whole of 2017!), **Golf Street Halt**, **Carnoustie** and **Arbroath ★★**. The last is home of the famous Arbroath Smokie, a fish wonderful if done well (and there's little more dramatic than the mobile smoking barrels some smokie sellers have). By the way, as we run up from Dundee, there are good views back to the bridge and Fife, exactly as there were on the south of Fife, but across a different firth.

If you were told this section was laid in Indian-gauge with rails 5ft 6in apart, you would be incredulous, as clearly normal British trains (which run on 4ft 8½ in track) would fall off. But this was true, because early railways were isolated stretches which no-one dreamed would form a network. Eventually the Dundee–Arbroath line had to be relaid.

Soon we are approaching Montrose. Before there, on the right, there's the picturesque ruin of Red Castle and behind it, Lunan Bay. In fact, there is a series of bays. They look inviting for a dip – but the water this far north is always achingly cold. Following this is an elegant viaduct at Ferryden.

RED CASTLE, LUNAN BAY

IAN HOLM, SHUTTERSTOCK.COM

77

'THE RACE TO THE NORTH'

The bitter rivalry between the two consortia of companies that operated what are now called the West Coast and East Coast Main Lines to Scotland in the 1880s and '90s was so intense that 'The Race to the North' broke out – to be the first to reach Edinburgh overnight, and, after the Forth Bridge was built, the first to reach Aberdeen. The event seized the public's imagination to the point where crowds would gather at the departures in London, and even in the middle of the night, at places like Carlisle. Fleet Street would send reporters to every major station en route to telegraph the arrival times. One railway owner, the Marquis of Tweedale, cabled his manager: 'Beat them at any cost!'

There was dreadful cheating with the signalman at Kinnaber Junction, where the two routes joined, being bullied or bribed to delay one or other company's train.

Speeds were such that passengers were hurled to the floor by curves. At Cupar in Fife a gang of workmen stood ready to put the track on one curve back three inches each time the express hurtled round it (or to help with the rescue if it didn't)! Eventually it was realised that lives were being put at risk and things calmed down. Still, with both routes to Edinburgh now wired up, how about a renewed race that would electrify the country, railway chiefs? Just the once – the publicity would be terrific.

Montrose*** is approached by an annoying (from a signalman's point of view) single-track section, over a rumbling bridge that crosses the mouth of Montrose Basin, an extraordinary stretch of water running two miles or more inland (to a place called The Lurgies, as it happens). 'Basin' is exactly the right word for this place, for after I looked across the broad expanse of water on the way to Aberdeen and wondered if it was deep enough for boating, I got my answer on the return train. The water had vanished, leaving a muddy waste riven by streams and gullies. If the tide is running as you cross the bridge, look at the piers of the parallel road bridge, and the water that eddies and swirls dangerously against them. I can think of places I'd rather be in a boat. So 'basin' is right – it's as if someone has pulled the plug out twice a day!

The station is perched beside the water, with the town crammed into the rest of the peninsula that almost encloses the basin. On leaving Montrose, look to your left across a field to see the embankment of a converging trackbed of a line that used to come round the north side of the basin, also heading for Aberdeen, just as we curve right. Of course there must have been 100 old trackbeds joining the line since we left King's Cross, but this is an important one, *Kinnaber Junction*, marked by the railway even today with a special signboard, and scene of the dramatic tussle between railway companies known as 'The Race to the North', a fierce 19th-century rivalry between the competing companies and routes (see box, page 78).

For **INVERNESS--ABERDEEN**, see page 143.

Now, just as happened in Fife, the railway gets bored with hugging the coast and lunges across country and easier farmland to race north, crossing one river on a high viaduct. There are mostly closed stations in this rural section, although we pass the recently reopened **Laurencekirk*** (most useless information in this chapter: famous for the Laurencekirk hinge, an airtight snuffbox closure).

We reach the coast again at **Stonehaven*****. Stonehaven itself is set down by the sea, a haven indeed. The short run along the cliffs to Aberdeen is a scenic highlight, similar to the coast near Berwick. As we leave, the view back to Stonehaven is highly recommended, across an old church and graveyard on this side of the town, and a castle on the other side. Sparks fly at Stonehaven on New Year's Eve with the Fireball Ceremony, where men march down the High Street whirling balls of fire on wire ropes. The blazing circles are startlingly dramatic.

We hurry along the cliff tops, impatient to finish the journey. There are spectacular views over the sea and down into dangerous foaming gullies and mysterious caves where the waves enter. We run through **Portlethen** station and down over a river into **Aberdeen**.

This tough city of oil-rig workers, sailors and fishermen and no-nonsense, no-frills bars has various attractions I can't list here (and an onwards journey to Inverness and the Highlands by train). The tourist people would rather talk of 'The Granite City', 'The Flower of Scotland', or 'The Silver City by the Golden Sands'.

I'd just point out two things: one of the platforms (probably the one opposite where you came in) has an ancient milepost under its lip, midway along, down by the rails. It says Carlisle 241, though there's no direct route to that border city and the distance is wrong by train nowadays. But there *was* such a route, and it was the main line, further evidence of 'The Race to the North' (see box, opposite).

The other oddity is down by the harbour, at Shore Lane. There's a business called the Shore Porters Society, established 1498. *1498?* No, they're not joking. This was set up just six years after Columbus 'discovered' America (well, Cuba) and the Old World hadn't yet decided whether to do anything about the New (or just cover it up and pretend it wasn't there). This firm was set up *centuries* before Australia and New Zealand were even thought of, and yet is still going as a removals firm. Remarkable, though not the oldest business in Britain, but that's another story.

South Beach, Troon (PAUL TOMKINS, VISITSCOTLAND)

Scotland Goes On Holiday

GLASGOW TO AYRSHIRE AND DUMFRIES

The **GLASGOW AND SOUTH-WESTERN LINE**, known locally to railwaymen as 'the sou-west', is a much under-appreciated route which – as it says on the tin – goes southwest from Glasgow. If you include the **AYRSHIRE COAST LINE**, it's in the shape of an upside-down Y, with Glasgow at the top, Dumfries and Carlisle (in England) bottom right (east), and the Irish ferry port of Stranraer (or more usually now via a coach link to Cairnryan) bottom left (west), so it's doubly international. There are a few fabulous branches off, with one route linking across the arms of the Y at about halfway – making England to Stranraer trains possible. However, most of the linking routes (including one right across the bottom, making a triangle) have long gone – more's the shame in the latter case.

THE GLASGOW & SOUTH-WESTERN MAIN LINE**

TO THE LAND OF 'OREO COWS' & A ROMANTIC ANVIL
2HRS 25MINS, 89 MILES

The route runs from Glasgow Central to Carlisle across the border, via Kilmarnock and Dumfries. Carlisle, of course, is also on the much quicker **WEST COAST MAIN LINE** (page 32), but this route serves a broad hinterland and has connections to the **AYRSHIRE COAST LINE** in the form of a link from Kilmarnock to Troon, and a branch to East Kilbride in the Glasgow suburbs.

The route was downgraded by British Railways after the main line to Glasgow was electrified, a massive mistake as it is still needed for diversions when the WCML route is closed and it's costing millions to put back each bit of double track. It does, however, remain a fascinating rail backwater and is a useful secondary route, speeding commuters and shoppers and football fans into Glasgow from the small towns it serves.

GLASGOW CENTRAL TO DUMFRIES**
1HR 45MINS, 86 MILES

Leaving **Glasgow Central** with all the other southbound routes, the train leaps across the Clyde – well it does if the bridge is still there – and the **INVERCLYDE LINE** and **AYRSHIRE COAST LINE** instantly split off to the right (west). We pass under a freight line and soon the **WEST COAST MAIN LINE** departs left (east) although, like us, also heading for Carlisle.

The **CATHCART CIRCLE LINE** (page 52) leaves or joins on both sides and after all that frantic junctionery we reach our first station, **Crossmyloof**

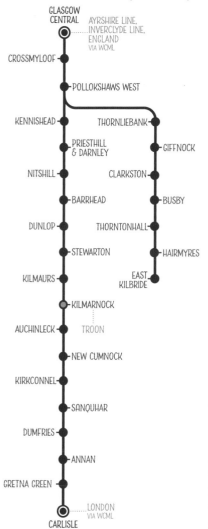

(just 1 mile 60 chains). What a brilliant name – said to derive from the Gaelic *Crois Mo Liubha*, meaning Saint (Ma)lieu's Cross. It's best to have a ticket arriving here, unlike a cow, which – despite the very urban setting – walked here in October 2012, having escaped from a country park. Despite the busy lines, she was somehow returned home unbarbecued.

Oddly enough, this escaping malarkey happened again in January 2020, when two 'highland cows' were spotted on the track south of here. ScotRail tweeted: 'We've had reports of a couple of Highland Cows on the railway line… We think they're on the run from Pollok Park… We'll get them moooooved as soon as we can. Thanks for your patience.' Any passenger who had a… erm… beef on that crowded morning that 'this train is like a cattle truck', well – that was exactly what was needed on that occasion!

Much further down the route near Dumfries watch out for 'Belties', a type of cattle properly called the Belted Galloway, which is black with a creamy-white belt round the middle. Young folk call them 'Oreo

THE 'OREO' COW: BELTED GALLOWAY

EWAN CHESSER, SHUTTERSTOCK.COM

cows', after the similarly coloured American cookie. Look out for them, they really do look like that.

We pass under the **CATCHART CIRCLE LINE** to reach **Pollokshaws West** after which, at *Busby Junction*, the **EAST KILBRIDE LINE** takes off left in a more southerly direction (we are heading pretty well west with a marked reluctance to head for England compared to the WCML!).

Kennishead (4¼ miles) **Priesthill & Darnley**, and **Nitshill** come next (followed by the striking St Convall's Catholic cemetery on the right), before **Barrhead** (7½ miles), which has a few more facilities and a north-facing bay for terminating trains. South of here the track was singled in the crazy economies of the late 20th century and is being expensively redoubled in stages. The train climbs hard for a few miles to a village called Uplawmoor on the left (no station) and after, the track redoubles at *Lugton signalbox*, great views open up on the right across to the mountains on Arran, often snow-topped.

Dunlop, set in rolling East Ayrshire countryside, was actually closed briefly by the Beeching cuts, but reopened after an outcry and even regained its second track and platform in 2009. **Stewarton** follows, often a blaze of colour in the summer with its volunteer flower planters. A blaze of a different sort happened

THE EAST KILBRIDE BRANCH

After leaving the South-Western Line, this unelectrified line serves **Thornliebank**, **Giffnock**, **Clarkston**, **Busby** (7¼ miles), **Thorntonhall** (8½ miles, single track by now), **Hairmyres** and **East Kilbride** (30mins, 11½ miles), Scotland's first post-war new town. If it is raining again, you will understand why Charles Macintosh invented waterproof coats here!

just south of here in January 2009 when an oil train fell through a weakened bridge on to the A735 road. Several wagons caught fire, but nobody was hurt, and after three weeks' closure the line was reopened with a much stronger bridge, you'll be glad to know.

Just south of the station is the elegant 555ft-long ten-arch *Stewarton Viaduct*, which arches crosses Annick Water.

Next comes **Kilmaurs** (which also closed in the bad old days and then reopened) and the grander station at **Kilmarnock**, just after the **TROON LINE** joins us from the right (west) with a signalbox in the V of the junction.

Kilmarnock has four platforms, a handsome clock tower, glazed canopy, café, gift shop and booking office. Change here for that connecting line to Troon, Ayr and Stranraer.

South of the station we cross the *Kilmarnock Railway Viaduct*, a low structure with 23 masonry arches that rather dominates the town centre, and indeed is sometimes floodlit at night as a feature. You get a good view of the town to the right. Don't be confused by tracks joining or leaving – they were mostly for freight. This was such an industrial area with collieries and ironworks all over the place, so lines and sidings that remain must be a tenth of what was here once.

We turn more southeast now, heading for England after all, cross another good viaduct near Crookedholm – talking about crooked, the massive Kilmarnock Prison is soon on the right, filled with people who might not be enjoying this view quite as much as we are. We pass through *Mossgiel Tunnel* (648yds) and, about a mile later, after passing the village of Mauchline on the left, cross the superb *Ballochmyle Viaduct*, the highest in Britain at 169ft (and the world's biggest masonry arch when built), then another bridge plus some lovely open country to reach **Auchinleck** (home of James Boswell, Samuel Johnson's biographer; see box, opposite).

Then it's across another marvellous viaduct at Cumnock, **New Cumnock** (another reopening), through bleaker country to **Kirkconnel**. A plaque at the station rightly commemorates poet Alexander Anderson, who rose from being a railway track-worker to become Chief Librarian at Edinburgh University (more on him on page 175). He wrote under the name *Surfaceman*, being another term for a plate-layer.

(Ermm… well that's not much clearer, what's a plate-layer, some may ask, a person setting out banquets or something? No, they were the hard-working chaps who laid and maintained track, once called plateways.) Mind you, this brainy fellow does put you in mind of the signalman philosopher, who really had ideas above his station… Always useful to have friends in high places, I suppose!

Moving swiftly on, **Sanquhar** follows (another welcome reopening, and a jumping-off point for the Southern Upland Way in this grand walking

THE JOHNSON WHO GOT SCOTS' BACKS UP – & WE DON'T MEAN BORIS!

James Boswell (left) was the somewhat put-upon Scot who traipsed around with the writer of the first proper English dictionary, Dr Samuel Johnson (right). The latter's sayings about Scotland are legendary but still guaranteed to get some people's backs up – and make some people smile – centuries later.

Johnson may have bullied Boswell or they may – like many a married couple – have got used to the cranky comments. And Johnson may have been obliged to say something quirky, memorable or outrageous on his travels to sing for his supper, as it were, like Oscar Wilde in the following century, or indeed Stormzy in the 21st.

Boswell quoted him saying: 'The noblest prospect which a Scotchman ever sees is the high road that leads him to England.' In his dictionary, Johnson defines OATS as: 'A grain, which in England is generally given to horses, but in Scotland supports the people.' But at the risk of having Tunnock's Teacakes thrown at me by angry Scots (actually that would be

quite nice, go right ahead!), wasn't there a bit of truth in both of those – I can't list all the Scottish bosses I have worked for in London, where they get on wonderfully well. But for a balancing view about London, see Dumfries (page 92). It was true about oats, but now the English have learned to also love this humble, healthy grain.

Not sure, though, that I can defend another Johnson remark – I think said purely to tease Boswell – 'Much may be made of a Scotchman, if he be caught young'. It was a joke, though no doubt offensive. But thanks, anyway, Boswell, for writing his biography – and thus immortalising both of you. And recording your grudging, drudging trudging around Scotland!

PS: You can see Johnson's dry humour in this dictionary entry (about himself): *LEXICOGRAPHER: A writer of dictionaries; a harmless drudge, that busies himself in tracing the original, and detailing the signification of words.*

85

country). We and the A76 follow the picturesque and curvaceous Nith Valley. Eventually we veer left and climb to a long tunnel near Enoch, then descend into farming country.

But why, you sensibly ask, didn't we, like the road, follow the Nith down on to the plains?

Well, the answer railway historians give is astonishing. Drumlanrig Castle (pictured opposite as you sadly won't see it from the train) is across the Nith Valley and home to the Dukes, and indeed Duchesses, of Buccleuch and of Queensberry, owners of about 120,000 acres of Scotland. More than one history states that the Duke insisted that the railway be hidden from his grand castle, once dubbed the 'Pink Palace'. This meant the 1,397-yard-long *Drumlanrig Tunnel* had to be built by a workforce of 600 using 7 million bricks, and has a couple of ventilation shafts emerging in brickwork on the hill above. To get the railway up to the tunnel, the 111ft-high *Enterkin Viaduct* with its four arches runs above Enterkinfoot and a huge retaining wall just to the north of the tunnel had to be built. Even the wall was famous for a time as the global benchmark of its type, carefully constructed by German engineers.

All this so just one Duke could keep his view? Actually it's not just one Duke – I recall the old duke driving up to a farm gate (in a very tatty old estate car) and chatting to a little girl. She asked: 'Is it true you are a duke?' He said – words to this effect, it's a long while ago – 'No, my dear, I'm two dukes.' And so he was. Still, two dukes though, must be rare. As a matter of conjecture, isn't he heir to the Duke of Monmouth too? That would make surely the only person on the planet who is three dukes!

This is no reflection on the current duke, the tenth and twelfth, who might even like railways and have a giant Hornby-Dublo trainset in his attic.

Still, I wonder if the correct form of address is Your Graces instead of Your Grace? Not that they need us to flatter, but the railway needs something flatter (what a terrible link – you may feel the writing, like the train, is going downhill fast!). We descend from the tunnel to a river plain, then cross the Nith again on a massive bowstring girder bridge – do look right close by the far end for some fantastical if not rather surreal landscape gardening and topiary.

DUMFRIES TO CARLISLE**
THE 'QUEEN OF THE SOUTH' & LITERARY NOBILITY
36MINS, 33 MILES

Eventually we cross the Nith one last time and curve left into **Dumfries**, a more spacious station with a café and some railway relics on display. Dumfries is an interesting town, known – as is its football team – as 'Queen of the South' and offering connections with long-distance cycle routes; see signpost outside station to give you some ideas. The nickname of the proud football team is 'the

THE QUINTINSHILL DISASTER

At the start of this book, I gave a list of superlatives about Scottish railways, such as highest, tallest, widest, longest – all wonderfully true. There's another one that could be added. Worst.

The worst crash in Scottish, and British, railway history. Now I apologise for mentioning it, and please stop reading this section if this kind of account upsets you, but in fact most people are fascinated by things going badly wrong. We remember the RMS *Titanic*, for instance, and what happened to her, but not her two sister ships which missed the icebergs. No-one makes a whole series of films about them!

So with that caveat in mind, and the assurance that you couldn't be on a safer form of transport than Scotland's railways today, and further that this section will *prove* how these things could not happen again, this is the story of the worst disaster in British railway history.

Just north of Gretna Green on the West Coast Main Line, just after the Dumfries Line has diverged to the west, is a spot whose name was seared into the memories of railwaymen, Scots and the military – Quintinshill.

It was early morning on 22 May 1915, in the midst of World War I. The British were rushing troops to make an expedition to Gallipoli with the hope of knocking the Ottoman Empire out of the war.

Quintinshill was a remote spot, named after one of the very few nearby houses, and the double-track main line had – and still has – two passing loops, one Up (towards London) and one Down (towards Glasgow), with the points and signals all controlled from Quintinshill Signalbox, the only railway building there. So to make it quite clear, there were four tracks

just for a long train length, and then points (switches in American) restored the main line to just two tracks, north and south. The whole system was groaning under the load of the war, shuffling vast numbers of coal trains north to the fleet at Invergordon and Scapa Flow, and extra troop trains too.

The purpose of such loops was, and indeed still is here and at other spots around the system, to let slow or heavy trains – such as goods trains, which in those days went as slow as 20mph – get out of the way of express trains. In other words, to allow overtaking. Sometimes a bit of shuffling was needed to make this work. As on this fateful day.

The 06.17 Down stopping train from Carlisle arrived and needed to get out of the way of two heavy express sleeper trains also heading north. It couldn't do the obvious thing and go into the Down loop, next to its own Down (northbound) track, as there was a goods train already standing there, so the signalman had the stopping train reverse via a crossover on to the Up (southbound) main line and stand there outside his signalbox. This wasn't unusual or against the rules, but those rules had to be followed very carefully.

A train of southbound (or Up) empty coal wagons, which had been held at a signal while the stopper reversed, was now allowed into the Up Loop. So now three of the four tracks were occupied by standing trains.

The first northbound sleeper hurtled through safely at 06.38. At this point the signalbox to the north – Kirkpatrick – offered the Quintinshill signalman a southbound troop train at 06.42. The latter forgot all about the stopping train standing there right in front of his box – with

two other trains – and set the signals for the troop train to speed non-stop right through to Gretna, the box to the south, with the 'line clear' message (all these were done by bell codes). Except that it wasn't clear. Immediately afterwards he accepted the second Down express, the 06.05 from Carlisle.

The troop train hit the stopping train head-on at 06.49 and the resulting pile of smoking wreckage blocked the Down main line too. The appalled signalman threw the lever to set his Distant signal for that line to danger, but the second northbound express sleeper had already passed it and a minute later smashed into the pile of wreckage.

You now had five trains piled up on four tracks and on fire with the dead and dying inside, and the carnage was all the worse because the troop train was formed of obsolete wooden

carriages – pressed into use because of the war – which were smashed to matchwood. They had outdated gas lighting, which meant more flammable material was being piped into the blaze – there were five steam locos with white-hot coal fires, some under there, remember. All five trains were largely consumed in the ensuing blaze.

At 06.53 the signalman sent the 'Obstruction Danger' bell signal to Gretna and Kirkpatrick signalboxes, stopping all trains. It was far too late, but it alerted the outside world that something untoward had happened.

The fire was so huge that all the tons of coal in the locomotives' tenders was consumed. As it raged through the piled-up wreckage, trapped or injured men begged others to shoot them, or shot themselves, and several accounts attest to that, although of course rifle cartridges ➤➤

←← on the dead men were going off in the flames. One BBC interview, mentioning this aspect many years later, was cut rather than broadcast.

It was difficult to be certain about the final death toll, so little was left of some bodies. It is thought around 226 people died and 246 were injured. The crowded troop train took the worst of it. There was a horribly grim roll call at 16.00 that day for the 500 soldiers of the 7th Battalion Royal Scots – only 58 men and seven officers answered the bugle.

The dead were buried in a mass grave at Edinburgh's Rosebank Cemetery (where there is a substantial memorial to them today). The public were kept away as the coffins were stacked three high. Four children's bodies were never identified and buried in Glasgow's Western Necropolis, as they were never claimed, one coffin pathetically marked 'little girl, unrecognisable'. Some experts now suspect they were the shrunken remains of soldiers. One survivor later claimed that a couple of perhaps reluctant or shocked soldiers made

off into the morning mist, knowing their identities would be lost.

There is another memorial at Larbert station, near Falkirk, from where the doomed troop train originated.

The amazing human errors – certain slipshod practices and the astonishing oversight of the relieving signalman forgetting about the presence of the train he had just arrived on, and the guards of two of the trains being in the signalbox (as per the rules to remind the signalman that the trains were there) while the mistake was being made – are all too complex to go into here. As is the believable theory (in my opinion) that it suited the railway company to have the signalmen blamed and jailed for manslaughter rather than face public outrage for their poor practices (otherwise why were they quietly given jobs with the same company again on their release?). You have to design out the chance of human error in such technologies or else it will eventually find you out.

There were so many grim aspects to this, and one happier aspect. One of the grim aspects is that the soldiers were heading

Doonhammers', which at least avoids confusion with the fairly recent Netflix TV series *Queen of the South*, which appears to be about a bunch of losers – not something the football team ever do, of course!

The station, which once had more routes east and west too – hence the spacious glazed area where those platforms have been filled in, and the gap between today's two where the centre road was for freights in busier industrial times – even has two valid claims to literary fame (and the town has at least two more, big time).

It features in the 1915 spy thriller novel *The 39 Steps* by John Buchan, made into a memorable movie by Hitchcock (and about 38 less memorable remakes!). Richard Hannay, fleeing German agents desperate to kill him, arrives here and changes trains for Galloway, where more adventures follow. And at the beginning of another war, T S Eliot published *Old Possum's Book*

for Gallipoli, which we now know was an appallingly mistaken campaign, and they would have there suffered similar casualties, equally pointlessly.

But perhaps we should also remember the few positives. This accident and a few others led to leaps forward in railway safety. The introduction of track circuits – where an electric current passes through the wheels and axles of trains – shows where trains occupy a stretch of line. Interlocking was developed, which makes it impossible to signal a train on to the occupied sections. Various safety devices make the brakes come on if anyone mistakenly tries to enter such a section. And last but not least, gas lighting and flimsy wooden carriages have long gone, and carriages got stronger and stronger.

Further up this same West Coast Main Line, at Grayrigg in Cumbria, a train crashed at much higher speeds on 23 February 2007. It was a Pendolino tilting train, and was doing 95mph when it left the tracks on some faulty points that had not been properly maintained. One person was killed, and of course that is appalling and totally unacceptable. But it was doing perhaps twice the speed of the trains at Quintinshill. None of the carriages collapsed or caught fire. It was tragic, and should not have happened, but 225 fewer people dying in a much higher-speed crash was a gigantic improvement.

That problem with the points maintenance was addressed and not one passenger on a train died on any British railway in more than a decade. Sadly, there was an accident near Stonehaven in August 2020, in which one passenger and two staff were also killed. A landslide had fallen on to the tracks. It ended that record super-safe period of 13 years with no passenger fatalities, but you can see the pattern of moving to far rarer accidents with far fewer casualties – while thousands died on the roads in those years. You really are pretty safe on a Scottish train.

That's how railways work, getting safer and safer. But at any rate, now you know the meaning to railwaymen and women of that terrible word, Quintinshill.

of Practical Cats, which features a charming poem about Skimbleshanks, the Railway Cat, who patrols Dumfries station every night. It gives a human touch to a somewhat austere, dry, I didn't say pompous, poet. I have, by the way, twice come across three-legged railway cats. It seems to be an occupational hazard.

Dumfries is well worth a stroll around – turn right out the station up Lovers Walk, and left at the top past Dumfries Academy, alma mater of *Peter Pan* creator J M Barrie and about a dozen other notables. Take a walk along the High Street to Midsteeple and see if you can spot the strange milestone that says: 'Huntingdon 272'. I mean, how many people in those days wanted to go from here to there in the average week? Erm... how about none?

Walk beyond down to the Nith riverside and cross by the ancient Devorgilla bridge or the suspension footbridge to the walk on the far side for a good view of the town. There is an updated museum at the Robert Burns Centre here and they have done a good job of making his words come alive centuries later. Recommended and free – as are his house in the town and two other museums. He wrote of this town, compared to London:

> The **THAMES** flows proudly to the sea,
> Where royal cities stately stand;
> But sweeter flows the **NITH** to me,
> Where Cummins ance had high command:
> When shall I see that honor'd land,
> That winding **STREAM** I love so dear!

Only three stations remain on our route. **Annan** is followed by a decent viaduct. It was also the junction for the now-forgotten Solway Junction Railway, which went straight to England across the Solway Firth on a long-gone sea-going viaduct (in order to get Cumberland iron ore to the Scottish steelworks more quickly).

The viaduct was poorly built and damaged by floating ice sheets, and a failure. For a while before being demolished it was used by Scots on foot willing to trek its 1½-mile length to get to pubs with English opening hours (in order to get English beer to Scottish stomachs more quickly). This kind of thing also happened in 'dry counties', where pubs closed earlier or all day on Sundays. One hopes they all made it back across the windswept derelict viaduct safely after their nights out!

Then we reach **Gretna Green** (another welcome reopening and redoubling), famously the site of a different sort of coupling than railway trains, as English couples eloped across the border to get married here under then more lax Scots law. Famously they forged their marital links – without parental approvals usually – over the anvil in the blacksmith's shop. No jokes please about a ball and chain!

The point where we merge with the **WEST COAST MAIN LINE** from Glasgow (coming from the left, with overhead wires) is only a few feet into Scotland, the English border being the stream, the River Sark, crossed immediately, not the much bigger River Eden 1½ miles further on that many folk on this railway, and the parallel M6 Motorway (which the Scottish M74 has suddenly become) assume is the border. We are close to the site of Scotland's worst rail disaster a little way north on the main line (the blacksmith at the famous forge in Gretna Green heard the smash and ran to help – see box, page 88). Then we are rapidly into **Carlisle**, still a bustling six-way junction and a fascinating town (see box, page 33). Change for the **SETTLE & CARLISLE LINE*****, **THE CUMBRIAN COAST LINE****, **THE WEST COAST MAIN LINE*** (north or south), and **THE NEWCASTLE–CARLISLE LINE*** (all featured in the sister book to this, *Britain from the Rails: A Window Gazer's Guide*).

THE AYRSHIRE COAST LINE**
I'LL TAKE THE TROON TRAIN!
2HRS 12MINS, 72 MILES

This coast is recreationally a perennial favourite for central Scotland, as it has great beaches, wonderful views, seaside resorts, more golf courses than you can shake a five iron at, the famous racecourses of Ayr and Troon, and ferry connections to beautiful islands. Plus it takes in two international airports. All aboard!

GLASGOW TO KILWINNING
24MINS, 26 MILES

Leaving **Glasgow Central** station, the first part with a few inner-city stations is shared with the Inverclyde Line (described on page 103) as far as **Paisley Gilmour Street**, where each route has its own two platforms. In fact, it is just before the station, at *Wallneuk Junction*, where the tracks diverge. Paisley Gilmour Street's entrance is in grand Scottish baronial style and is a listed building, and it's Scotland's fourth-busiest station – alight here for connecting buses to nearby Glasgow Airport. If you stay on the train, note the frosted-glass windows on the waiting rooms alongside – almost Paisley pattern! There are three other stations in the Renfrewshire town. The interesting (disused) church spire on the left (south), which is a hollow collection of arches, is what the English call a 'Scotch crown'.

The Ayrshire Coast trains speed southwest past three long narrow lochs on the right (west) – Castle Semple, Barr and Kilbirnie – or maybe not if you have caught the stopper, which halts at **Johnstone** (note that beautifully slender spire on the right (north) of the high Parish Church), **Milliken Park** (we are now reaching proper countryside), **Howwood** (amid wind farms, the first of many today, harvesting something of which Scotland has infinite supplies) and **Lochwinnoch** (and 1½ miles later, if you like a wee dram,

GLASGOW CENTRAL
GLASGOW & SOUTH-WESTERN LINE, ENGLAND VIA WCML
PAISLEY GILMOUR STREET
INVERCLYDE LINE
JOHNSTONE
MILLIKEN PARK
HOWWOOD
LOCHWINNOCH
GLENGARNOCK
DALRY
KILWINNING
IRVINE
ARDROSSAN AND LARGS BRANCHES
BARASSIE
TROON — KILMARNOCK
PRESTWICK INTERNATIONAL AIRPORT
PRESTWICK TOWN
NEWTON-ON-AYR
AYR
MAYBOLE
GIRVAN
BARRHILL
STRANRAER

1

2

3

JAMES MCDOWELL, SHUTTERSTOCK.COM

KENNY LAM, VISITSCOTLAND

KENNY LAM, VISITSCOTLAND

1 The famous Devorgilla bridge in Dumfries **2** Luce Bay **3** Pinmore Viaduct
4 Sunset over Ardrossan **5** Dumbarton Castle, across the Clyde **6** Gourock

spot the piles of whisky barrels on the left and the Chivas Regal plant). Then comes **Glengarnock** and **Dalry** to the junction for the coastal towns at **Kilwinning**. Because all the routes stop here, this is the busiest station in Ayrshire, with four platforms. If continuing south to Troon, Ayr and Stranraer, skip the next section.

ARDROSSAN & LARGS BRANCHES*
26MINS, 16 MILES

This route swings west away from Kilwinning and the main line, to which another short, electrified curve connects southwards to make a triangle at *Dubbs Junction*. We reach the first of the 'Three Towns' conurbation along this bit of Ayrshire Coast at **Stevenston** (useless fact of the century – this area was once famed for producing more Jew's Harps than anywhere else, now renamed in more politically correct times as 'mouth harps'), with its level crossing, then pass loads of holidaymakers' mobile homes (what a misnomer, they never go anywhere!) to reach **Saltcoats** (famous for once producing, ermm, salt) on the coast, whose station retains two decent 19th-century buildings. **Ardrossan South Beach** follows, where only one platform is in use, and then at *Holm Junction* the short 1-mile branch diverges left (west) to **Ardrossan Town** and **Ardrossan Harbour**. This connects with the ferries to the Isle of Arran.

If continuing towards Largs, the train climbs up the hill (how does it do this with the track next to us clearly unelectrified – I know you worry about these things – well, the wire continues unseen above us on this single track only, so the other line is now a great long freight-only route).

And it gives us sensational views across the sea to Arran, then calls at **West Kilbride**, passing huge industrial sites, which formerly gave the railway a lot of business, and goes to **Fairlie** through *Fairlie Tunnel* (1,004yds) and into the seaside resort of **Largs**.

An unusual appearance in the Main Street taxi rank outside on the early morning of 11 July 1995 was a 107-ton Class 318 train from Glasgow Central, which had failed to stop, crashed through the buffers and the ticket office, severely damaging the station building, and demolished two shops before coming to a stop.

No-one was killed and the station buildings were replaced, with stronger German-made buffers. These are now painted bright red to help the driver see the darn things. Still, there is a good argument for not standing up until a train

LARGS

KENNY LAM, VISITSCOTLAND

has stopped at a terminus – it's the one place you are likely to hit anything, yet everyone stands up! It does happen once in a very rare while, and has entered the language, after all, in the expression about a project hitting the buffers. Or as the makers of these ones might say, *Achtung, Prellblock!*

Arriving in far more stately fashion, we note the station has two platforms and space for a 'centre road' – where steam engines were released to run round their trains in the old days. A marvellous garden has been built on old sidings alongside – which is where sidings tend to be – and refers to the Viking stories of Largs, which is proud of having repulsed Helgar the Horrible or Olaf the Obnoxious and their chums back then. So proud, in fact, that a Viking ship burning is part of the annual Viking Festival (it's a big event with parades held at the end of August/beginning of September).

They might also tell the story of how the humble thistle became Scotland's national flower. The naughty Vikings were creeping up on a Scottish coast fort in the dark, barefoot to avoid making any noise. One stepped on a thistle and cried out – and the Scots raised the alarm and threw Olaf and chums back whence they came. Is it true? Who knows. Maybe Angus mentioned the need for a national flower and Hamish said: 'Thistle do, Angus.'

In the town is the ferry terminal for Cumbrae, a quiet island only a mile offshore if you fancy a peaceful walk or cycle. During the first Covid-19 lockdown in 2020, police searched a van on this ferry and found a group of golfers aiming for some sport on the island. We shouldn't laugh given the severity of the pandemic, but it was all a bit Bertie Wooster. Stowaways in plus fours, old chum!

Don't miss Nardini's ice cream parlour along the front to the right (north) a way. It's the perfect Art Deco building inside and out and the ice creams are to die for (literally, I feared, after guzzling one, but it was that funny brain freeze you get from eating ice cream too fast). They also have a pizzeria that I haven't tried but you know what, the Italians might just know a thing or two about these.

In fact there's a great tradition of brilliant Italians in central Scotland, and such names pop up all over the place. Wasn't there a great sculptor Paolozzi? A late lamented singer called Zavaroni? A more recent chart-topping singer Paolo Nutini? A great painter called Vettriano? (Well, to be honest with the last named, he was called Jack Hoggan when raised in Fife, but he took his mother's name professionally. But you get the idea).

Anyway, the Nardini family also gave us the popular Bafta-award-winning actress Daniela Nardini, star of *Waterloo Road* and a lot more.

I did note a higher proportion of fish and chip shops than anywhere I've ever seen on the way back to the station. (Or fush and chups, in my poor imitation of a Glasgow accent.)

Best walk it off with a very pleasant stroll left (south) to the pencil monument (a tall pillar) and the large marina. Sensational views across the Firth of Clyde to all those interesting islands. It's just beautiful. Almost as beautiful as a Nardini's Knickerbocker Glory.

A new station, possibly called **Largs Marina**, may be added at the southern end of the town in next few years.

KILWINNING TO AYR**
BACK ON THE MAIN LINE
24MINS, 15 MILES

Staying on the main line south, we cross the Garnock Water to reach **Irvine**, a new town based on an ancient borough, and birthplace of Scots First Minister Nicola Sturgeon. Superb views open up on the right of the mountains of Arran and Ailsa Craig.

Next station down the coast is **Barassie**, where a linking line from Kilmarnock on the Dumfries line to Carlisle trails in from our left (east). That line used to have two platforms of its own but they have closed, although the line is well used – it makes it possible to run England to Stranraer boat trains (or to Ayr for Cairnryan), and a local service operates on the route, often from Kilmarnock to Stranraer. The odd name for our next stop, **Troon**, probably comes from the Welsh/Pictish for the nose, referring to the shape of the land. Golf heaven, I'm told.

The first Troon train to reach here, in 1812, was the Duke of Portland's horse-drawn line from Kilmarnock. This was not authorised to carry passengers, so to get around this, passengers had to be weighed and charged as freight items. More on the history on page 3. The harbour is to the right (west), and note the lovely station clock on that side (and a useful shop/café).

Next is – as the fuel sidings on the right and the landing lights on the left suggest – **Prestwick International Airport** station (45mins, 37¾ miles), which directly serves what is now called Glasgow Prestwick Airport. A spot revered by some as it was the only place Elvis Presley set foot on British soil, on 3 March 1960. The King of Rock 'n' Roll was in uniform after finishing military service but was already well known enough for a crush of fans to seek autographs. This is quickly followed by **Prestwick Town, Newton-on-Ayr** (and judging by the loved-up couple across the aisle on my train there should be a station called Walking-on-Ayr – I got the impression he'd proposed in Troon) and across the River Ayr to **Ayr** (1hr, 41½ miles), which is a grander affair with four platforms, two being through ones and two being bays facing Glasgow. The station building and canopy are still attractive but at the time of writing the adjoining station hotel was derelict, but listed, and indeed for a while the danger of it collapsing caused much of the station to be cordoned off. I hope this is cleared up by the time you reach there.

AYR STATION

PAUL TOMKINS, VISITSCOTLAND

FIND THE CHIEFTAIN OF THE PUDDING RACE

From Ayr you can visit the Robert Burns Birthplace Museum, about a mile (maybe 20 minutes' walk) due south of the station, on Murdoch's Lone, Alloway.

There isn't space to do the man's poems justice, but merely to remind you that these two lines often jokingly said to refer to haggis...

> Wee, sleekit, cow'rin,
> tim'rous BEASTIE,
> O, what a panic's in thy breastie!

...are actually from a typically humane 1785 poem entitled *To A Mouse, On Turning Her Up In Her Nest With The Plough*. Well worth a close read!

We can find Burns's actual words on the subject in Bradshaw's 1863 Railway Guide. Bradshaw says [here Burns] 'wrote his spirited lines *To a Haggis* –

> Far fa' your honest sonsie face,
> Great chieftain of the
> PUDDING race!

Bradshaw feels the need to explain to travellers: 'A haggis is a pudding exclusively Scotch, but considered of French origin. Its ingredients are oatmeal, suet, pepper and onion, and it is usually boiled in a sheep's stomach. Although a heavy, it is by no means a disagreeable dish.'

There's a fine war memorial on the hotel side, and another more recent one on the opposite platform, because of the danger of that hotel collapsing during the annual wreath-laying, which would probably be a sacrifice too pointless.

Note that Ayr is where foot passengers for Cairnryan ships to Northern Ireland alight for a road coach transfer, as the ships no longer directly connect at the end of the railway at Stranraer.

ON TO STRANRAER***
THE NIGHT THEY SAW RED WITH THE 'BLACK SHEEP'
1HR 24MINS, 59 MILES

Over the next 10 miles, keep an eye seaward for views of the dramatic island bird sanctuary of Ailsa Craig – home to 36,000 pairs of gannets, we are told by those who know. Well, I hope they've counted them – there might be the odd one, not in a pair, bit of a loner, less gregarious. Sits by himself on the cliff. Still eating like a gannet, obviously.

Continuing south, now on unelectrified single-track (so if you were on an electric train, you'll have had to change to a diesel coming probably from Kilmarnock via that linking line to Barassie), we reach **Maybole** a little inland, pass an isolated signalbox and loop at Kilkerran level crossing, then swing back nearer to the coast at **Girvan** (known to whisky tipplers for its Grant's distillery, the white buildings on the right just before the town). Girvan station is a listed 1950s building and signalbox, and is well kept by local people.

Back before World War I, a steam-engine driver called Davie Smith came to an embarrassing stop here with a terrible old loco No 74, 'the black sheep of Ayr'. Despite its awful state, he would make up lost time on the downhills by driving like a madman. He was known for 'driving furiously through the darkness until those big rough men were crying for mercy' (according to David L Smith in *Tales of the Glasgow and South Western Railway*).

They gave old Davie a mere cleaner to fire the engine one night, and the boy's face was soon 'as white as a cloot'. Tearing down towards Girvan the terrified boy yelled out: 'Canny on, canny on! There's a rid signal.'

With a great screeching of brakes the train was stopped. It turned out to be otherwise. Nor was he the first to make this mistake. The local crews knew this trap for the unwary. 'The Girvan men used to lie abed at night and hear them away up by the waterworks, whistling for the light of Girvan pier.' A 'red signal' was in fact that light out in the darkness of the Firth of Clyde that was never going to change. One suspects that words were had with the cleaner lad that night that may have taught him that lesson too.

At the time of writing, the various passing loops on this line had old-style signalboxes with proper semaphore signals and those tokens that the driver has to exchange by leaning out and grabbing (and letting go) with the signalman. It's an old system but very safe – you can't go up a line or set the signals without the right one, so head-on crashes are impossible.

Just after the station, we climb steeply up *Glendoune Bank* towards *Pinmore Tunnel* (543yds) – at 1 in 54, this is steep for a railway, especially from a standing start. Next we pass over the fine and slightly curved *Pinmore Viaduct*, by which we cross over the A714 road and the River Stinchar whose valley both road and railway are borrowing. There are grand views to the left (east).

After another high viaduct we reach **Barrhill** (passing loop on this single-track line) which, unlikely though it seems, featured in the Dorothy L Sayers detective novel *Five Red Herrings*. We are in far emptier country than those Glasgow suburbs back there, changing to sheep farming and then to moorlands, leaving roads and rivers behind. We climb again to *Chirmorie Summit*, the highest point of the whole route, and also the border between Strathclyde and Dumfries and Galloway. Here you can see (left, east) The Merrick, which at 2,766ft is the highest peak in southern Scotland. It is part of the Range of the Awful Hand (appropriately, as the mountain's name means 'the finger'). It sounds like something from a Hammer Horror film but is probably one of those things where the meaning has changed – it may have originally meant awesome or awe-inspiring. From the summit, the 144-mile line of sight to Snowdon in North Wales is theoretically the longest in the British Isles. I say theoretically because I've never heard of anyone actually seeing it (it would have to be pin-sharp clear). You can see both from

WOULD A RAILWAY TO NORTHERN IRELAND FROM SCOTLAND MAKE SENSE?

We are roughly an English Channel's width away from Ireland at Stranraer, or rather at Portpatrick, on the far side of the peninsula, where the railway used to end. Could it not be joined up by a bridge, as Tory Prime Minister Boris Johnson suggested in 2019?

Well, while most engineering challenges can be done if there's the will and the money, there are two good reasons why this shouldn't be done. Not simply because of how deep that waterway is, and how stormy, but because of what is in the bottom of those deeps: explosives and poison gas shells, dumped there after the two world wars.

They tried taking trains of 32 wagons of gas shells down the Stranraer line, or rather on a branch to Cairnryan docks via a now long-gone junction. Then some clever clogs in the War Office thought it would be more economical to double the length of the train, with the result it was uncontrollable on a downhill.

As David Smith recounts in *Tales of the Glasgow and South Western Railway* of one unfortunate driver: 'He couldn't stop, ran past the home [signal], through the loop, burst the points at the far end, finally pulled up just past the starter [signal], then in a panic – for he thought the 10pm "up Paddy" was in section [the express coming from Ireland] – set back and sent four wagons of gas shells all over the road.'

Thankfully they didn't explode. But as he remarks in some understatement: 'I think 64 [wagons] of poison gas behind your tender and you can't stop is quite enough excitement for any normal driver for quite a time!'

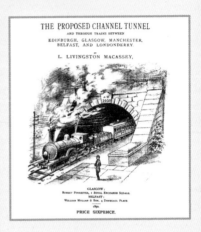

THE PROPOSED CHANNEL TUNNEL
AND THROUGH TRAINS BETWEEN
EDINBURGH, GLASGOW, MANCHESTER, BELFAST, AND LONDONDERRY.
BY
L. LIVINGSTON MACASSEY.

GLASGOW:
ROBERT FORRESTER, 2 ROYAL EXCHANGE SQUARE.
BELFAST:
WILLIAM MULLAN & SON, 4 DONEGALL PLACE.
1890.
PRICE SIXPENCE.

So besides the explosives and poisons filling the trenches where they would have to build bridge piers three times the height of the Shard in London, what's the other reason a rail bridge to Ireland is not a good idea? This misgiving applies equally to the tunnels proposed several times in the late 19th century.

To put it simply, the trains would fall off the rails when they got there. Britain and Europe have a track gauge of 4ft 8½in, made popular by the Stephensons, but actually set by a Roman horse's bum. As mentioned elsewhere (more details on page 43), if you take a horse's bum and set shafts down each side to an axle and then set chariot wheels outside them, you have around that width, as can be found in rutted Roman wagon ways. If you put flanges on a Roman chariot, you could run it into Glasgow Central.

Ireland, on the other hand, built its lines – for its own good reasons, no doubt – to the same gauge as the Grand Duchy of Baden State Railways: 5ft 3in. Too wide!

England's Scafell Pike, though – along with the Isle of Man and Northern Ireland. Five countries in one view!

Another 'box and loop comes at Glenwhilly amid moorland – what an isolated job manning the signals up here! It would suit some people, the bleak beauty. The station that served a few farms has long closed, and just south of this is a tightly curved section of railway known as 'the swan's neck'. The trains coming up from the sea – called 'the 10 o'clock Paddy' by railwaymen back then because of coming from Irish ferries – sometimes didn't make it up the bank and had to be split in half, with the engine coming back for the rest!

We speed down attractive Glen Luce and glimpse the sea, Luce Bay, to our left (south) but then turn sharp west to Dunragit (probably stopping for the token, but no station) for the last few miles into **Stranraer**, alongside another inlet of salt water, Loch Ryan. We are crossing the shaft of a hammer here – the long hammerhead being the romantically named Rhins of Galloway, a 25-mile-long otherwise isolated chunk of land containing many farms and on the left end, seen as we approach, the southernmost point of Scotland, the Mull of Galloway. There was a port used earlier for boats to Ulster on the far side – called Portpatrick, and the railway went there too once – but it faced directly into the Atlantic storms. Which are not to be trifled with – a whole ferry went down here in January 1953. But nature had thoughtfully provided a very sheltered deep-water haven round the side. Not long ago they went from this town but now go from Cairnryan, a few miles up the loch by bus or taxi.

Clearly all the railway sidings and docks sitting at Stranraer are waiting for long boat trains and ferries that will probably never come. As one local said, the ferry terminal move knocked the stuffing out of the town. Well we came for the superb ride, and if you stroll into the quiet town for lunch it's not a bad place with a good pub or two, some curious shops, and this unique train service. It was well used on my return ride.

By the way, I suppose the correct term for a narrow strip of land joining what would otherwise be an island to a mainland is not a hammer shaft but an isthmus. In which case, may I be the first to wish you all a merry isthmus!

THE INVERCLYDE LINE TO GOUROCK*

IN THE TRACKS OF HEROES
38MINS, 26 MILES

The demand for a railway to Greenock, down the Clyde towards the open sea, came about because the Clyde paddle steamers took a couple of hours to do a journey which a railway could do in less than an hour. The rich wanted to reach their weekend villas on the shores of the Clyde more quickly. The working people wanted quicker access to the resorts down the coast on the 'trades holidays'. Even poor emigrants were carried down this line on their last journeys on Scottish soil to waiting ships.

Starting from **Glasgow Central**, there are 21 stations. Soon we pass *Shields train depot* on your left (east), with dozens of trains in the attractive ScotRail saltire livery (or maybe another colour if another company has taken over – lemon yellow for Caledonian, maybe?). If you are football mad, keep your eyes peeled right (north), for Ibrox, home of Rangers. Next come **Cardonald, Hillington East, Hillington West, Paisley Gilmour Street** (a much grander structure, see page 93), along the *Underwood Viaduct* to **Paisley St James** (which football fans want renamed Paisley St Mirren after that other stadium visible on the left), **Bishopton** (site of a Roman fort in the Antonine era – everyone recalls Hadrian's Wall but there was an Antonine Wall too, this far north. In another conflict, World War II, this was the site of an ammunition factory), followed by a pair of 300-yard tunnels (*Bishopton No 1* and *No 2 Tunnels*) hewn out of solid rock, as the dramatic cutting between

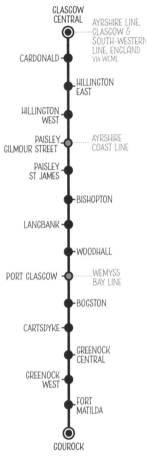

them shows. Then comes **Langbank**, note fabulous views across the Clyde to Dumbarton Castle on its rock before **Woodhall**, **Port Glasgow** (junction for the **WEMYSS BAY BRANCH** (page 62), which climbs off to the left) where all trains stop, giving a five-trains-an-hour service, **Bogston, Cartsdyke** and **Greenock Central** (the original terminus). Then through short *Ann Street Tunnel* to **Greenock West**, and through *Newton Street Tunnel* (longest in Scotland at 2,111 yards, unless you include the longer Glasgow subway) to **Fort Matilda** (the well-preserved station buildings are partly used by the local model railway club, but the Napoleonic-era fort has long gone) and to **Gourock**, completing the Gourock branch in 1889. Here ferries leave for the popular resort of Dunoon across the Clyde on the Cowal Peninsula, a heck of a long way round by road.

As a display at the station rightly reminds us, this area has a heroic wartime history. The German submarine U35 was sunk in 1940 north of Ailsa Craig by HMS *Gleaner*. The Russian convoys assembled in the anchorage known as the 'Tail o' the bank', which is where the Clyde expands into the Forth of Clyde (and there's a pub of that name on the shore here). Some 783 ships sailed that perilous journey past enemy-held Norway – with 87 merchant ships and 18 warships lost with most of their crews.

Churchill left Greenock Pier for those talks in America with Roosevelt. As did the disguised dead body of 'Major Martin' in *Operation Mincemeat* (the greatest deception in military history, detailed in my book *Madcap Military Mayhem*).

The great Clyde-built liners – the Queens *Elizabeth* and *Mary* – sailed from here as troop ships, journeying alone because they were the fastest and biggest in the world. *Queen Mary* did one round trip of 118 days out from the Clyde carrying 28,900 troops in various legs – and covering 37,943 miles.

And, crucially, the total of American troops who disembarked here in May to December 1944 was a staggering 1,317,089 – the biggest such troop movement in history, without which D-Day could not have happened. And, of course, those who survived had to be taken back home again in 1945 from ports such as this.

It's a lot to think about as you look around the waterfront, and wander up Kempock Street. If you get one of the sea-facing window seats in the cafés or pubs along here, or beyond, it's one of the best views in the world. Seriously!

Of course, you could try the open air swimming pool at the end of the road. It looked lovely – but as it was November, I gave it a miss and headed back to the pub.

BORDERING ON THE BRILLIANT!

The Borders Railway

One of the many things to love about Scotland – besides the sensational scenery, wonderful whisky and the tendency to deep-fry anything that stands still for a moment – is their staunch belief in railways. Somehow they fought off many proposed Beeching cuts in the 1960s that suggested, for example, uneconomic lines north of Inverness be closed (which meant all of them). Had they been in England or Wales, they surely would have been. One route that was in fact closed in that infamous era, the Waverley Line through the Borders, has been brilliantly brought back to life as the Borders Railway.

The new name better reflects what it now does, and the nation isn't as obsessed with Sir Walter Scott's novels, the source of the original name, as it once was. Nevertheless, it runs from Edinburgh's station named after his novel *Waverley* – next to the magnificent Scott Monument on Princes Street – to the literary giant's glorious home Abbotsford on the banks of the Tweed (page 112). You can't get more Scott-ish than that!

The rebuilt line was opened by HM the Queen, no less, riding the Royal Train behind an A4 steam loco (the same class as glorious world-record holder *Mallard*) on, fortuitously, the exact day when HM became Britain's longest reigning monarch: 9 September 2015. Both the monarch and the Scottish-owned loco, *Union of South Africa*, were looking pretty darn good for their age (89 and 78 respectively), and the crowds flocked to see two legendary old ladies who had not run out of puff.

They also flocked shortly afterwards to ride the new line, not surprisingly, given that level of publicity, so the usage exceeded targets – a million passengers in the first year instead of the envisaged 650,000. The number of carriages has often had to be increased because of overcrowding. So get to the termini a bit early so you can find a nice window seat, rather than risk having

THE BORDERS RAILWAY

1 Passing the Gala River 2 Stow 3 The disused station at Melrose on the Waverley Route
4 Abbotsford House, home of Sir Walter Scott

to stand (as you might do during the Edinburgh Festival, for instance), and wait by the doors if they are not open yet.

The original Waverley Line went right through to Carlisle, and I believe it will be extended further south soon. Certainly there are towns that would benefit – Melrose is only a mile further, and Hawick. Meanwhile, here's how to enjoy today's route.

Borders Railway services run pretty well half-hourly. A canny thing was done in rebuilding this railway. There wasn't the money, demand (so they thought, wrongly), or space to build it all double track, so they put in what they call 'dynamic loops'.

Instead of short loops for oncoming trains to pass each other, meaning they have to stop, these are a few miles long so they can pass at line speed. It sounds like a recipe for chaos, because any train running late would delay others. In fact, on my trips several trains sped past going the opposite way, so normal passengers would have assumed they were on an ordinary double-track railway – unless they looked down and saw the other track was missing most of the time. This bit of ferroequinological choreography – to coin a phrase – works surprisingly well most of the time, and don't worry, it has fail-safe technology to halt any trains over-running their loops!

SOUTH FROM EDINBURGH*
HOME ON THE GRANGE
1HR, 35 MILES

Starting going east from **Edinburgh Waverley**, as if heading for London King's Cross, we pass through the tunnels under Calton Hill, and if you look right there's a view of Arthur's Seat (hill), and in front of it, the bottom end of the Royal Mile running from the castle behind us. Here you can see one probable reason why these tunnels went through this hill rather than taking the line a few hundred yards further south and round it – the towers of Holyroodhouse, the monarch's Scottish palace (whence HM in the opening ceremony mentioned previously started her procession to the station). Bagpipes coming past the royal bedroom window might be acceptable – even desired, we are told – but not blastpipes on the 07.51 to Newcastle, so the railway was kept away.

On the right soon is *Craigentinny depot*, where interesting odd locomotives and railway vehicles are always to be seen. This is busiest at night, when it takes in perhaps 15 trains belonging to various operators, plus odd locomotives – say 120 rail vehicles – which all need servicing, small defects fixing and major repairs such as engine or wheel changes done by skilled engineers, plus cleaning, fuelling, watering and readying for the morning. The unseen part of railway operation.

We then part company with the **EAST COAST MAIN LINE**, which diverges left, and reach **Brunstane**. Then there is a triangular junction on the right with the *Edinburgh Suburban and Southside Junction Railway* which runs across the south of the city to near Haymarket in the west, avoiding congested Waverley. This 'South Sub' is used for freight and moving empty stock around, but notwithstanding my earlier praise for Scotland's railway policies, for reasons I can't fathom, the several stations on the route remain closed as no regular passenger trains have used it since 1962. Come on, Edinburgh, you've spent hundreds of millions on trams, yet this line's there, ready to go!

Unlike, it must be said, the Borders Railway a few years ago – which had to be relaid and even rebuilt at several places where the A7 road, also heading for Carlisle (and also doing so by heading somewhat the wrong way to start with – a bit east of south), was earlier modernised by unhelpfully obliterating the railway formation.

Next comes **Newcraighall**, **Shawfair**, and **Eskbank**, followed by the new *Hardengreen Viaduct* over the A7, and then the substantial *Newbattle Viaduct*, a restored 23-arch structure where we run down the middle of a former double-track formation to even out the load (as with the famous Ribblehead Viaduct on the S&C in England). Next is **Newtongrange**, where provision for further redoubling of the track has been made, **Gorebridge**, and then now in more rural surroundings we climb steadily to the 880ft *Falahill Summit* (you'll notice the engines stop labouring when we are over the top and running down beyond). You can perhaps see why this was the one cross-border route that closed – in steam days it was a struggle to get heavy trains up the 1 in 70 gradient. To put it another way, you could hear it for miles around when someone was coming up with the goods.

It's the tenth-highest standard-gauge rail summit in Britain, and only 36ft lower than the once-notorious Shap Summit on the WCML. But as there, it's no problem for modern trains, passenger or freight.

ONWARDS TO TWEEDBANK**
A GALA AFFAIR

Beyond the summit is the best bit, scenically. We run down the Gala Valley, crossing the sparkling Gala Water several times, with only **Stow**** an occasional stop. Look to the right (west) in a broad valley for Borthwick Castle, remarkably well preserved (because it surrendered quickly to Oliver Cromwell's artillery). Here in the previous century Mary Queen of Scots had been besieged and escaped disguised as a page boy. Now it's a posh marriage venue (much recommended – the venue that is: you must make your own mind up about marriage; just try to do better than poor Mary!).

BORTHWICK CASTLE

DUNCAN2406, SHUTTERSTOCK.COM

This is followed by a couple of tunnels and we arrive at **Galashiels**, a textile town that is capital of the Borders, at a station squeezed into a hillside because a supermarket encroached on the old trackbed. The council did, however, build a useful bus interchange across the road which helps integrate transport to the outlying areas.

The town name means 'dwellings by the Gala'. The scene of fortifications and raids since Iron Age and Roman times, the town features a great statue of a border reiver (lawless raider – the word is related to ruffian) on horseback, and the town's coat of arms makes a hidden reference to the violence of those days – an apparently innocuous picture of a pair of foxes looking up at a plum tree with the date 1337 and the motto 'Sour Plums' (sometimes said and written Soor Plooms).

It refers to the day some English soldiers were surprised while picking plums out of a tree here. Don't be tempted to pick any – those visitors ended up in an awful jam!

Onwards over the gorgeous River Tweed – which for many miles is the border, but not here – on the *Redbridge Viaduct*.

Tweedbank is a new station and in keeping with the somewhat parsimonious provision at times along the route was going to be a crummy one-short platform terminus with a bus shelter. Late on in the construction phase some bright spark realised it could be a terminus for steam and other excursions, so two full-length platforms and a set of points to connect them were provided

111

THE INNOCENT RAILWAY

Why is there an 'Innocent Railway' line – mostly disused – in Edinburgh? It's not like England's 'Virgin Viaduct' (crossing the River Wharfe at Tadcaster), which was so-called because it was built but never used by a train – this line was heavily used by trains from the start. Some say the nickname is a reference to the fact that trains on this route, the Edinburgh and Dalkeith Railway, were horse-drawn, so the track was not defiled, as it were, by noisy, smelly steam locomotives. Not true, although it was such a horse-drawn line to start with. Others claim the title refers to the fact that the line – or group of lines – never had an accident. Not true. Or a fatal accident, then. Again, not true.

The line was opened very early in the railway age, in 1831, to bring coal from the Dalkeith pits to the capital then known as 'Auld Reekie' because of the smoke that rarely stopped belching from chimneys. The line – laid to Scotch gauge (4ft 6in between the lines) came from the southeast and skirted the south side of Arthur's Seat, ending in St Leonard's. A 550-yard steep tunnel was needed to reach the terminus, which is today one of Europe's oldest railway tunnels. Ropes, not horses, pulled trains up to the top of the tunnel.

Extensions to the coast made the very early line attractive to Edinburgh folk, who had never ridden a railway before – and horse-drawn or not, the line to the seaside was soon busy with carriages. It was a huge success both for bringing coal more cheaply to the capital and for passengers taking holiday trips.

The possible real origin of the name was mockery that the railway was so slow and simple. Trains would stop anywhere anyone asked to get on or off.

Dr Robert Chalmers is said to have coined the intriguing name. He wrote in that early years:

'In the very contemplation of the innocence of the railway you find your heart rejoiced. Only think of a railway having a board at all the stations forbidding the drivers to stop by the way to feed their horses! By the Innocent Railway you never feel in the least jeopardy; your journey is one of incident and adventure; you can examine the crops as you go along; you have time to hear the news from your companions; and the by-play of the officials is a source of never-failing amusement.'

– hence the Royal Train and steam loco made it thus far. And it will be useful when the line is extended, as it surely will be.

There isn't a lot at Tweedbank, to be frank, mainly a park and ride place for Borders folk, but there are two great options for further exploration. One, walk a mile to Walter Scott's fascinating house, Abbotsford, or check beforehand with the shuttle bus that meets a few of the trains (see 🖱 scottsabbotsford.com).

Or second, and this I recommend, make a day or an afternoon or evening or a night of it and walk ahead on the line of the track, then bear left at the end down to the bank of the Tweed. Walk on through lovely countryside for less than a mile and when you seem to encounter civilisation again bear

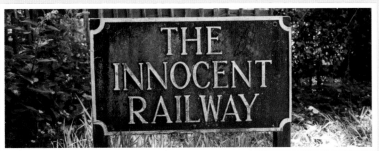

In fact, it was adapted to steam traction, from the 1840s, and to a track gauge that matched the national network.

Part of the route became the Waverley Line (today's Borders Railway), and a little bit goes under today's East Coast Main Line. So when Richard Branson's firm took an interest in the latter route in the early 21st century, the Innocent Railway appropriately welcomed Virgin Trains.

Today the route near Arthur's Seat is part of a long-distance foot and cycle path, including that tunnel.

A notice advises wayfarers: 'You are standing on one of Scotland's pioneering railways. The Edinburgh and Dalkeith Railway was nicknamed "The Innocent Railway" because it was originally horse-drawn in an age which thought steam engines dangerous. It was built to transport coal from the Dalkeith area to Auld Reekie. To the surprise of the promoters, however, the public rapidly took to this convenient novelty and soon 300,000 passengers were carried annually. Thereafter, passengers became as important as freight to the railways. Open carriages, wagons and converted stagecoaches were the first rolling stock. Among its engineering features were an early tunnel, a cast iron beam bridge and an outstanding timber viaduct on masonry piers. The first two still survive. The viaduct at Thornybank, Dalkeith was finally demolished in the 1960s.'

Now there are no stinky cars or lorries anymore – just walkers and cyclists. The railway route has regained its innocence.

right – it's lovely Melrose. Here is the gorgeous Abbey with its amazing stories (see *Eccentric Britain*), a pretty footbridge across the Tweed, the three Eildon Hills inhabited by secretive mountain haggises that dart among the heather and bracken (I was told), plus good pubs, restaurants and places to stay. The hills were known as Trimontium to the Romans, who attacked Pictish troublemakers at Galashiels, and were later home to a 13th-century local Nostradamus, Thomas the Rhymer (clever old timer).

So why not stay over in Melrose and spend half a day walking up these gentle peaks for splendid views? It'll be bordering on the best excursion you ever had!

THE WORLD'S MOST SCENIC RAILWAY
THE WEST HIGHLAND LINE

*****
5HRS, 164 MILES

This is simply the most spectacular railway journey in Britain – and for that reason, it is the only railway in this book (and indeed, its sister book, *Britain from the Rails*) to which I assign five asterisks. If you like landscape, prepare to be enthralled. But don't expect it to be quick, and ideally don't do the whole of it both ways in a day unless you have the stamina of an ox or can sleep on trains. It is possible, and I've done it gladly, but it's a long day.

However, you can stay in nearly all the places up this wonderful route, as well as extend and vary the journey by ferry or by bus. And this isn't just a great line for scenery and railway buffs; active types can bring (or hire) bikes, tents, canoes and boats; the hiking is superlative; and outdoor activities are all over the place. Pack midge repellent in late summer/autumn if you're doing the outdoor stuff.

Oh, and it's also starred in many films. *And* offers a superb steam-train ride. What are you waiting for?!

GLASGOW QUEEN STREET TO CRIANLARICH*****
FROM LOWLAND BUSTLE TO EMPTY HIGHLANDS IN A FEW MILES
1HR 50MINS, 58¾ MILES

The transformation that this route makes is simply staggering. You can't believe it's on the same trip. In London terms, it's as if there were a totally empty wilderness round about Croydon or Harrow. From bustling, industrial city with ugly tower blocks to real Highland bleakness and scenes of bewitching lochside beauty, it really is a special experience.

I'D SIT ON THE LEFT UNTIL LOCH LOMOND – AND THEN CHANGE IF POSSIBLE TO THE RIGHT. NO MATTER IF YOU CAN'T.

We soon leave the suburbs and pass through a station called **Singer** (where the sewing machines were made, employing 5,000 in the world's largest factory), stop at **Dalmuir** and get a great view of the Clyde Road Bridge, in a

LOCH LOMOND

kind of suspension design. We then come down to the shoreline and parallel the **WEMYSS BAY BRANCH** (page 62) on the far bank.

A call at **Dumbarton Central** and we cross the wide and fast-flowing River Leven (which drains Loch Lomond, not so far away to the north) before, about 23 miles out, at *Craigendoran Junction* we swerve right off the electrified **NORTH CLYDE LINE** to Balloch and start climbing on single track, the start of the West Highland Line and the start of real adventure.

Helensburgh Upper means there's a lower station on the other line, which happens again later in very odd circumstances; but we have the Upper hand there too.

Soon we get splendid views of Gareloch on the left across the Clyde to Greenock. In May, we are in bluebell-strewn woods, a peaceful place – odd given that for most of the past 40 years the loch down below has been a nuclear missile submarine base.

At **Garelochhead** we meet the first of many passing loops, and take the right one, perhaps in deference to the ships in the loch below which like to pass port to port. The station's doubtless higher up the hill than the villagers would like, but then the West Highland Line is fighting for height. We cross a high viaduct and then power through a rock cutting, emerging on a hillside with views of Loch Long – and no human habitation. Don't you suddenly feel you're reaching the Highlands? Rhododendrons thrive here, being Himalayan immigrants.

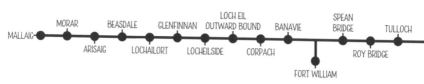

We climb higher and higher above the water, and then turn up Glen Douglas away from the loch. Now things are bleak and we *are* definitely in the pukka Highlands, still only haggis-chucking distance from Glasgow.

We reach a passing loop and some strange Ministry of Defence sidings, then emerge once more high above Loch Long – not a place to derail (which has never happened, I hasten to add!). There's a village and caravans viewed on the far shore as if from a plane.

Arrochar & Tarbet station often has timber being loaded. Suddenly we get a glimpse of a loch on the right, and fresh water this time. It's not *any* loch either, but the beautiful, legendary Loch Lomond, whose bonnie, bonnie banks we follow for miles. IT'S WORTH CHANGING SIDES TO THE RIGHT IF YOU CAN. You'll never get such a good view from the road, twisting even more than the railway below us, plus if you're driving you'll be watching those bends not the peerless scenery. No, this is definitely the way to do it. You can even read guidebooks!

There's a hydropower station, but it's discreet, not spoiling the indisputably bonnie banks of Loch Lomond. The largest expanse of fresh water in Britain, the other end goes almost back south to Dumbarton where we crossed the outlet a while back.

At **Ardlui**, we're told it's *officially* beautiful: we're in the Loch Lomond and Trossachs National Park. The latter are the hills. We veer into Glen Falloch, climbing and climbing, a great viaduct in a fantastic bit of railway building 143ft high above the river, and there are good views down to the river with a waterfall and strange-shaped boulders. Soon we reach **Crianlarich** (tea rooms, loos), with mountains all round, the biggest being Ben More, 3,843ft, to the east. Sometimes here there will be a train carrying massive aluminium slabs from the Fort William smelter waiting for the single line southwards. All the way up this route, you'll see no traditional signals, by the way, but blue lights that flash when it's OK to proceed – a radio-controlled electronic version of the tokens seen on the Aberdeen line. It's as safe as houses, I'm told; if a train drives over the grids on the track without possessing the token (displayed in the cab) for that single-line section, the brakes will come on.

Result: dozens of closed signalboxes along this line, and a massive saving in costs. It seems a shame in employment and heritage terms, but it may have saved this route. The lovely **OBAN BRANCH** peels off left here and our train may divide for part to go each way. For the absurd story of its connection, and the route you can take today, see page 131.

CRIANLARICH TO FORT WILLIAM*****

A LUCKY HORSESHOE, THE LAST GREAT WILDERNESS & A GORGEOUS GORGE

1HR 50MINS, 64½ MILES

We take off, after the Oban line leaves us to the left, across a viaduct and up Strathfillan (meaning 'valley of the Fillan').

We pass a holy pool in which they used to test 'lunatics' by binding them hand and foot and tossing them in to see if they would come up with a pebble from the bottom (yes, it was crazy) and soon reach **Upper Tyndrum** (see remarks on the Lower in the Oban section, page 132). Note how the original station buildings are still there, insanely large for the one or two walkers who join the train, and useless because they're all locked up. Let's hope they find a use for them before the vandals get there.

Talking of walkers, this is on the West Highland Way long-distance path which, like us, heads from Glasgow to Fort William. It's a terrific route if you're a Pennine Way-type of person, and there's a fairly easy-looking section on the left as we head north. But of course suitable clothing, footwear, precautions, maps, torches, first aid (and helicopter, mobile jacuzzi and self-heating madras curry), and telling people where you're going beforehand (and at some length afterwards), are all necessary before you start yomping all over the Highlands. I'm told some runners have done the West Highland Way in one go – 95 miles!

Tyndrum, by the way, was the centre of Scotland's not large gold industry, and the Crown Jewels (correctly the Honours of Scotland) were made from Tyndrum gold.

Pure visual gold is the totally perfect horseshoe curve coming up. Look ahead when you curve right at around milepost 44 (they are the yellow things on the left). You can see a piece of track heading north about half a mile away, but we will take two miles to get there, because we swerve right (east) into a perfect glacial valley, turn north around the end of it on two natty viaducts and then charge west up the other side to resume the course we were on. It's beautiful, framed by massive mountains, though you wouldn't have needed much more viaduct to carry straight on! The builders had run out of money and had to economise (hence so few tunnels between Glasgow and Fort William – one, I think). They simply went round obstacles in great curves. It's our gain – one of the best horseshoe bends you can see. Most countries' railways have at least one, but few as clear as this or as dramatically framed.

Bridge of Orchy comes next, with the station being used as a bunkhouse for trekkers. We leave the road which diverges left and start climbing fast for the most amazing bit of railway: Rannoch Moor, a true wilderness, a bottomless bog into which the railway nearly sank without trace.

This massive, high-level, treeless, roadless bog was almost as unknown as the surface of the moon when the railway was built, one of the last great empty wildernesses of Europe. True, a few men had ventured in there but some of them had drowned in the mire or, lost, frozen to death. We leave the road to pick a different route through the mountains and are all alone on a single-track line to doom (well, Mallaig, but it *feels* that lonely).

Talking about lonesome, *Gorton Loop*, which is next in the roadless middle of nowhere, would once have had a signalman living in a hut or two, with no way in or out but by train. Even water came daily by train, and once a year Father Christmas arrived on a special with a brake van full of toys for the railwaymen's children in isolated spots like this.

There are remains of old snow fences from here on; early trains were stuck for days but perhaps global warming, or more powerful snowploughs, have fixed that problem. Usually.

FOR PEAT'S SAKE: RANNOCH'S GREED

Getting up to Rannoch Moor at either end was a miracle of engineering. Building a railway across the 20 miles of bleak, treeless, roadless, impassable bog of Rannoch needed more than a miracle. Men and horses would drown in the quagmire. There were no paths, and travellers would get lost. Skeletons of lost navvies were found later on. The great road builder Thomas Telford had been up here to consider what seemed to him, too, a logical route. He looked at the place and gave up.

The railwaymen tipped stone from cuttings blasted elsewhere into the mire. They tipped and tipped thousands of tons, and no bottom was secured – the stuff kept disappearing, swallowed up by the malevolent moor. They sent to Glasgow for trainloads of ash. That all disappeared into the bog too. They couldn't give up because so much money had been spent bringing the line up to this place on either side, and money was running out.

Then someone seems to have remembered what George Stephenson did with the world's first inter-city railway, the Liverpool and Manchester line, 60 years earlier. He had exactly the same problem at the bottomless Chat Moss, and solved it by laying a raft of bundles of logs and brushwood, plus layers of turf, and then building the line on top of that. The raft sank, but it floated down there and held up the stone roadbed for the line. For all I know, the bundles of logs and twigs are still there – the peat preserves everything well. You can feel the train sway and, if you are on foot, the ground move.

The only alternative was to dig great pits down to something solid, keeping out the mire with boarding, and make a stone viaduct pier, which is what they did in a depression north of Rannoch station for 684ft. It must have been right mucky work.

Rannoch Moor (BRUCE GALLOWAY)

An early 1894 guide to the line says of this 20-square-mile, 1,000ft-high moor: 'Monotonous it certainly is to the pedestrian… but from the window of a railway carriage it is the reverse of wearisome. There is an infinite solitude in its vast and open expanse that renders it a spectacle never to be erased from the memory…' Exactly, old chum.

Rannoch station (tea room, accommodation) was also in a spot cut off by impenetrable bog, but now has a road that was built by the railway. There's a

THE *JACOBITE*: GET ALL STEAMED UP

FORT WILLIAM–MALLAIG, 41 MILES; USUALLY DONE AS A ROUND-TRIP DAY OUT WITH TIME AT GLENFINNAN & MALLAIG, FROM AROUND 10.20 TO 16.00

This is Britain's most successful main-line steam service, and no wonder. It goes from one beautiful place to another through sensational landscape, the line itself being part of the spectacle, as well as the train. There are proper steam whistles, the roar of safety valves making waiting children jump, the *chuff–chuff–chuff–chuffchuffchuff* as the wheels slip on wet days. The clickety-clack of traditional Mark 1 unpowered coaches with that gentle shwooshing of the brakes downhill, huge windows actually lined up with the seats, windows that actually open (a miracle nowadays) to God's good air, more likely God's good steam and smoke, and slam-doors with drop-windows for photographing through. Brilliant.

It's not too long for a family outing, it's affordable, and it's reliable. It's also in a holiday area where people want this sort of day out. The West Coast Railway Company, based in Carnforth in Lancashire, have been running it every summer and if they can keep steam alive where so many others have failed, good for them.

The engines aren't the tiny tank engines seen on some preserved lines, and they don't do those pathetic speeds either, but carry on doing a proper job over a decent distance, complete with sweaty blackened fireman and driver, much like they used to have. Yes, it's nostalgia for more innocent times when dirty smut meant something in your eye. Mind you, it had its comic moments when a loudspeaker announced 'this is a non-smoking train'. At that very moment the engine was laying a huge duvet of grey and black smoke in the sky about 500 yards long.

A word of warning to those not used to this era of trains. Don't lean on the doors (they open outwards). Don't let your kids get their hands trapped in them (they are not called slam-door trains for nothing). And don't lean out of the windows to get that perfect shot on the camera/video. You will not see the lump of rock or tree branch on this limited-clearance line. The picture will be posthumously viewed by your relatives, and the Health and Safety brigade will probably have the windows sealed up.

I even got to go on the footplate (they don't let everyone). When I stepped down, my carbon footprint was left on the platform. Marvellous. For contact details, see page 180.

carving at the north end of the face of Renton, the man who saved the line by donating money in the last months of construction, and who drove the last spike joining up the two ends. The cheering navvies were so pleased they grabbed a boulder and with their tools set about carving his likeness, which is still here.

As we leave there's a good view east (right) down over Loch Rannoch. It's a strange thought that not far beyond the end of that loch the lonely road snakes over a hill to the Highland Main Line round about Blair Atholl. A stiff walk – or about five hours and umpteen miles by rail, via Glasgow, Stirling and Perth.

There are wild deer frequently now, big enough to dent the front of the train. What seems to be a tunnel is in fact a snow shelter. It had a removable middle section which in the summer would let light in and smoke out. In Norway they still have heaps of these on their railways. We climb now in snaking movements to lessen the gradient. I would swear we're still floating on that raft of logs from the tipsy roll of the train.

At **Corrour** (walkers' hostel) is the 1,347ft (410m) summit of the West Highland (in fact it's just north of the station and well marked with signs). Read John Thomas's wonderful book on this line to hear how the early morning 'ghost' freight from Glasgow once slowed at the summit to pick up the tablet and took off rather too briskly down the other side. The result was that the guard's van, which had not reached the summit at the rear of the train, snapped off – with the guard snoozing beside the stove. It rolled backwards with signalmen at Rannoch, Gorton and Bridge of Orchy not daring to derail it for fear of hurting the sleeping guard, who dozed on despite swaying alarmingly over viaducts and screeching round curves. Eventually a worried stationmaster tracked it down, stopped by a rising gradient, and woke the guard and told him where he was. 'Impossible!' he exclaimed, 'we were there two hours ago!' He had rolled back 20 miles.

Corrour station gets a role in the hit film *Trainspotting* (more about mainlining drugs than trains, so don't look for *Flying Scotsman*. They wanted somewhere bleak. Here it is!). The engines get a well-earned breather (as did the fireman stoking in steam days), and now the brakes need to guide us somehow down to sea level again – and what a totally superb ride it will be!

We take swooping downhill curves, looking to lose height and soon encounter the treeline again. We emerge high above Loch Treig, whose beauty was totally unknown to the public before the railway came here. We turn right along its shore, but hundreds of feet above the water, and follow a remarkable route on a rock shelf, sloping a full five miles down to the water level far below. I've been told the hillside route has 160 bridges and culverts to carry the streams – every one of which must be cleared lest a washout takes the line away – but I'm afraid I haven't counted them for you. You can check the mileposts, however, as we go down – it's 73¾ at the top and 78¾ at the bottom, so it really is a five-mile slope. Meanwhile you have plenty of time to admire the can-do Victorians –

THE WEST HIGHLAND LINE

BUCCHI FRANCESCO, SHUTTERSTOCK.COM

SUPERSTOCK

MOUNTAINTREKS, SHUTTERSTOCK.COM

PHILIP BIRTWISTLE, SHUTTERSTOCK.COM

ALAN KRAFT, SHUTTERSTOCK.COM

MENNO SCHAEFER, SHUTTERSTOCK.COM

AIRBORNE LENS, VISITSCOTLAND

1 The end of the line: Mallaig **2** Loch Awe **3** Ben More **4** The dramatic bridge at Connel Ferry
5 Neptune's Staircase, Fort William **6** West Highland Way **7** Highland cow – och aye the moo

contemplate the hostile opposite shore, for example – who looked at a bit of wilderness and just said: 'We can build a railway here.'

Now we are safely at the bottom, I can tell you that a train *did* come off the rails on the line high above Loch Treig in 2012. A freight loco hit a rockslide in a blinding rainstorm, and hurtled down the slope towards the loch. To the relief of its driver, it didn't turn into a submarine, but stopped on a shelf. He was rescued by helicopter. After months of deliberation about how to get it out – a fairly new Class 66 worth seven figures – it was decided it was cheaper to write it off, take out any useful components and cut it up on site, all done in 2013. The loch luckily didn't live up to its Gaelic meaning – loch of death – but do those legends tell us anything? The loch's legendary monster, an 1893 book related, would 'tear any interloper into a thousand pieces with his teeth and trample and pound him into pulp with his jet-black, iron-hard, though unshod hoofs!' How many pieces did the Class 66 end up in, I asked a railwayman. 'Round about a thousand…'

After a short tunnel comes **Tulloch** (to where the wheelsets of that wrecked loco were rolled after recovery). Then keep your eyes peeled left for another scenic treat, the Monessie Gorge. You look down into fantastically carved stone cliffs, eroded by the swirling peat-brown water that's just begging to be made into whisky. It's signed helpfully from both directions. Gorgeous.

Roy Bridge station building was for many years used as a chapel, there being no other provision for the few inhabitants. There are fantastic views on the left in the next stretch, with the bulky Ben Nevis behind Fort William. Britain's highest at 4,406ft, like Everest it is not dramatically pointed from any direction. We cross another river, with the water pouring over massive rock strata pointing upwards. It's only a few hundred years since men looked at these and pondered: if the world was created as it now is, why jumble it up like this? The forces involved in twisting it round like this must have been gigantic.

Spean Bridge is followed by an unaccustomed fair lick of speed into **Fort William**. Notice on the right the **MALLAIG LINE** trailing in to meet us behind the signalbox. AS WE REVERSE TO GAIN THAT LINE AT FORT WILLIAM, YOU MAY WISH TO SWITCH TO THE OPPOSITE SIDE, FACING THE OTHER WAY TO CONTINUE.

FORT WILLIAM TO MALLAIG*****
OUTRAGEOUS BEAUTY & CONCRETE EVIDENCE
1HR 20MINS, 41 MILES

We leave the town on the shores of Loch Linnhe and head along the waterside. A rare case of old-style signalling exists here – or did last time I was there! – and splitting semaphores (that is two) tell us which route we're taking – the road to the isles or Glasgow. This time we pass on the other side of the

This is a truly, **TRULY** terrific journey, and for

HOW TO DO IT BY STEAM, see box on page 122.

signalbox then across the River Lochy. On the hills to the right are the massive pipes of a hydro-electric scheme, used by Alcan to make huge aluminium slabs, each capable of making thousands of rolls of kitchen foil. You may have seen some being hauled in the daily train south, and it's another thing that helps keep this line open, along with timber and some oil.

Next is **Banavie**, which was the end of a short branch line before the Mallaig Extension was built. I said there weren't any more signalboxes beyond here. I lied – there is this one, not only the control centre for all radio signalling, but also guarding the swing bridge over the Caledonian Canal, presumably because boats can't be detected by track circuits. That and the fact that you don't want a train ending up in the water, which happened surprisingly often in America, but not here. There's a truly massive bolt beside the track down on our left, worked by the signalman, which keeps the bridge in place. Nevertheless, there's quite a 'bong, bong' when you go over the gaps.

A MAN, A HORSE & A HORSESHOE: CONCRETE EVIDENCE?

The fantastic, beautifully located Glenfinnan Viaduct, on a picture-perfect horseshoe curve, is allegedly haunted. It contains a macabre secret, or so local lore has it. The viaduct was a radical experiment by 'Concrete Bob' McAlpine but during construction in 1900, the story goes, a horse and cart fell through planks into one of the hollow piers. So there you are rounding the curve at the foot of impossibly beautiful mountains, with a dead horse sealed beneath you. Bizarre, if it's true, but no-one has ever found it (and some say it is in the next viaduct).

The viaduct has been used in a few films, such as in *Harry Potter and the Chamber of Secrets* where an old Ford Anglia swoops around the train. The *Hogwarts Express* in that story, you may recall, starts at an invisible Platform 9¾ at King's Cross. Ridiculous fantasy – it would be

Euston, of course, to get to the West Highland.

'Concrete Bob' McAlpine went mad with his new material in the same way the Forth Bridge went mad with new steel, a few decades earlier. There's concrete everything up this line – a line which saved his life as he was rushed to hospital when badly injured. There's a museum about him and this place at Glenfinnan station after the curve. And note the pillar in the flat glacial valley we are curving around – it's a memorial to Bonnie Prince Charlie, who made this place famous by raising his standard here on 19 August 1745. Romantic hero or yet another dithering Stuart loser, you decide. The views down the valley to Loch Shiel are, however, undeniably superb, and the great concrete viaduct is in sight long before and after on the curve.

Do look right (landward) on the bridge to see Neptune's Staircase (designed by Thomas Telford in 1822), a great flight of locks which could just as well let Nessie escape as the sea god enter.

If you've ever looked at a map of Scotland, you'll have seen a gigantic slash running from here northeast to Inverness and the Moray Firth, as if God had sliced the Caledonian ciabatta with a galactic knife. Given that, it was an obvious way for boats to avoid the long and dangerous trip round the top of Scotland, and with Loch Ness, was already half-filled with water. It would also have been an easy way to get a railway to Inverness, and indeed a half-hearted attempt was made from Spean Bridge which reached halfway and then closed. It's a shame, because it's a mindboggling, but very rewarding way round by rail through Glasgow. However, there were almost as few passengers as monsters.

Corpach follows with a bunkhouse in the station. The place name means, those staying there may not wish to know, 'field of the dead' – nobility were kept there en route to burial on Iona. The canal basin is on the left, and there are good views back to Fort William and Ben Nevis when the clouds clear. We follow the shore of Loch Eil, and indeed **Loch Eil Outward Bound** with hearty youths building rafts, etc, confirms the area's outdoor theme. The deciduous woodland near ✋ **Locheilside** in late spring has carpets of bluebells (albeit a full month later than the south of Britain, but all the lovelier for that). We leave the A830 road to Mallaig (we rejoin later) and start climbing furiously. Next comes a highlight of highlights, with a stunning view that many judge as the best railway vista in the British Isles: the iconic *Glenfinnan Viaduct* (see box, page 127).

Glenfinnan station has a museum about the line, and a dining car (the steam trips stop here for about 20 minutes on their outward journey). Then there are overbridges, still standing in Concrete Bob's original material, and a dramatic rock cutting ends in a tunnel, followed by fantastic views to the right when we come out high above Loch Eil. The road has taken the further shore, so we are alone for several miles of great beauty, with waterfalls all around. Bonnie Prince Charlie hid in a cave here after his 1746 defeat.

The wooded islands are just lovely, and would look good in a Japanese painting. Who needs the Lake District or, indeed, Switzerland? Forests of these trees once covered this land in the great Caledonian Forest – until timber extraction and sheep farming got rid of them.

The sharp curves often have check rails (an extra rail to prevent derailment turning into a disaster), you'll be glad to know. We cross the river draining the loch and there's a request stop at ✋ **Lochailort**, where during the line's construction there was a shanty town of 2,000 navvies, complete with hospital and shop.

More tunnels, a sea loch, Loch nan Uamh, to the left, curving and climbing very steeply, isolated Polnish Chapel on the left (it was featured in the

movie *Local Hero*), more viaducts (concrete of course) and tunnels, then ✋
Beasdale, a request stop (because a local bigwig paid for it to be added as an
extra station). A tunnel and viaduct lead us to **Arisaig** (Britain's most westerly
railway station) with a fine old signalbox, a station building in concrete,
milepost: concrete, platforms: concrete. Concrete Bob's legacy! Did the staff
get paid in concrete, eat concrete sandwiches and use concrete loos?

There's a lovely view of a sea loch and over to the islands on the left (Rum,
Eigg and Muck, which sounds like a recipe for a hangover cure. Eigg is the
long flat one with the towering Sgurr peak at one end. Ferries to the islands
go from Mallaig). Soon we are seeing white-sand beaches with Skye beyond.
Another viaduct, descending to cross a peat moor, and **Morar** has not only a
1,000ft-deep loch to the right, but also a beautiful view to a bay on the left. The
films *Local Hero* and *Highlander* were partly shot on the beaches here. That
freshwater loch is, by the way, not only Britain's deepest lake – you could hide
the Eiffel Tower in it with 33ft to spare – but is deeper than the seas around
Scotland, until you get off the continental shelf beyond St Kilda. The River
Morar, which drains it, is among Britain's shortest.

And then we're there: seagull-squawking **Mallaig**, as far as rails could
possibly reach on the rugged West Coast, you may think. Until you discover
the Dingwall–Kyle line.

THE OBAN BRANCH***
AWE-INSPIRING RUINS, A ROCK PIANO,
THE MAGICAL ROUTE TO MULL & THE HOLY ISLANDS
1HR 12MINS, 43 MILES

The Oban line is just enchanting, and were it not for the exalted company it
keeps – the West Highland and the Skye lines – it would be the best, most
remote, and it could put in a good claim for the loveliest. I'D SIT ON THE LEFT.

Finished in 1880 as the Callander and Oban Railway, it was an entirely
separate route by a different company striving to get to the West Coast. It
crossed the West Highland at a right angle just after **Crianlarich**, where our
train divides from that bound for Mallaig. You can see the arch for the old
line in the bridge of the Mallaig line to your right. A spur from one line to the
other was put in for freight, but as the quarrelsome rivals fell out again a piece
of line was removed to make it unusable, and not restored for three years. It
was 35 years before Oban line passengers' pleas for a direct service to Glasgow
were heeded. Until then they had to scramble from one station to the other
and train times seemed designed to prevent any useful connection.

Meanwhile the old route was earmarked for closure in the 1960s, but nature
did it first with a landslide in Glen Ogle.

So this history explains why there are two stations at the next stop, **Tyndrum**, ours being Lower, the other Upper. It's given many a holidaymaker fun trying to race between the two to catch the train on the other line (which can usually be gained at a more relaxed pace by staying on to the junction at Crianlarich).

You can walk from one to the other easily in ten minutes, and you can cut out some of the road by taking a path marked by an old rail (on the way up) or turning left by the white bungalow (on the way down). You could even go by train from one side of the village to the other, if you're bonkers. I did this and it took an hour and nine minutes and 11 miles, via Crianlarich. By the way, if Waterloo Station was Britain's busiest station with 84 million passengers in one recent year, Tyndrum Lower was the least busy with just 17 (and one was me)! However, it's probably bad statistic-keeping, for a local tells me he's seen about a dozen passengers in one day.

Soon comes **Dalmally**, and a mile or so further keep an eye out on your left for a most romantic view of a ruined castle on a promontory sticking out into Loch Awe. Look how it guards the loch entrance with the opposite promontory; we cross the entrance river on a viaduct. **Loch Awe******** station is soon right on the water's edge. There's an old coach parked there which has been a tea room recently. The road keeps us company along the shore for miles now and the charming wooded islands are just too *Swallows and Amazons*-ish to be true. Loch Awe is awesome, but we can't see the full extent of the loch because we're following one short arm. The main run southwest is more than 20 miles.

Next is ✋ **Falls of Cruachan******** a summer-only request stop, handy for a tour of the underground power station. This is a line without traditional signalling and signalboxes, so the two-faced semaphores high on the left are a surprise. The strange signals all the way along here are controlled not by the signalman but by rock. They are connected to a set of wires running all along the hillside, nicknamed 'Anderson's Piano'. Any rockfall triggers a pair of signals to fall to 'Danger' showing each way. The apparatus is on the right, like a weird wired fence. It would probably be done with lasers nowadays, but there's no electricity in this fantastic contraption. Mind you, it must be a devil to reset if a demented deer crashes into it.

A train that did derail here in 2010 hit boulders which fell outside the 'Anderson's Piano' protection, proving that the contraption is needed, rather than that it didn't work.

OBAN

PHILIP BIRTWISTLE, SHUTTERSTOCK.COM

We leave the loch behind, following the river which drains it, and cross a superb high viaduct over the River Awe, descending west as we are, and after **Taynuilt** loop and sidings we soon reach the seawater again (on the right) where fish farms can be seen in Loch Etive.

The dramatic bridge at **Connel Ferry** can be glimpsed ahead on the right – we stick to this side of the water. It was an odd hybrid road–rail bridge where road traffic had to stop to allow trains across on the now-closed branch line to Ballachulish. It was shut so long ago that you can now only just make out the joining embankment after the station. Come to think of it, why couldn't they do this at Dornoch – just inset the rails into the bridge?

Down and down through woods and rock cuttings to **Oban*****, an achingly beautiful harbour, where the friendly red-funnelled Caledonian MacBrayne boats await to take you to Mull, thence perhaps to the holy island of Iona, cradle of Scottish Christianity in the British Isles. Or trips to Fingal's Cave, which so inspired Mendelssohn. It's a beautiful scene – not always so in winter though; islanders take refuge in Oban hotels during great storms.

Recommended is the Perle Oban Hotel (🐭 perleoban.com), the old railway hotel in front of you as you leave the station. It's not in the least bit fuddy-duddy, being modern, spacious and luxurious. Get a room with a harbour view, if you can. Perfect. If you can smell kippers in the breakfast room, I apologise. It'll probably be me.

SUMMIT SPECIAL
THE Highland Main Line

3½HRS, 118 MILES***

This route is spectacular, speedy by Highland standards, useful and never, ever boring. The description here starts at Inverness. Reverse lefts and rights if coming from the south. At times it is a double-track speedy main line, and at others a single-track mountain railway that twists through rugged country.

INVERNESS TO PERTH***
ALONG BRITAIN'S HIGHEST RAILWAY
2HRS 10MINS, 118 MILES

Leaving Inverness's curious triangular railway station behind, we take the left set of lines at **Milburn Junction**, unlike the Aberdeen route. This seems wrong but is soon rectified as we soar over that route.

Immediately we start climbing and climbing. There are fabulous views across the Moray Firth though soon we are ascending through woodland. We reach the great **Culloden Viaduct** with a slight curve to the west, then the A9 road, which we will be seeing a lot of today, crosses us.

This spectacular 1898 viaduct has 28x50ft stone arches, and one leaping 109ft across the River Nairn. Its brilliant engineer, Murdoch Paterson, was born at a farm a few miles from here and he died here too, while supervising its completion. It is said that his last request was to be pushed across the nearly completed viaduct on a trolley. Shades of Brunel and the Tamar Bridge!

Culloden Moor was, of course, the site of the battle that finished Bonnie Prince Charlie's 1745–46 rebellion. Whether it was a good or a bad thing for Scotland in the long run that he lost must be debated elsewhere, but don't let tour guides mislead you with talk of 'the English side' and 'the Scottish side'. There were more Scots on the government side than the rebel one. What is indisputable is that this moor was soaked with much blood, sweat and tears that terrible day. It's worth noting if you are rail touring Scotland, that the other end of Charlie's dream was at Glenfinnan on the Mallaig line.

You may miss it, but we soon cross a somewhat smaller but very rare timber-trestle viaduct of five spans. It is probably the last remaining one in Britain – the others having been replaced after rotting away. This is, amazingly, Paterson's 1897 *Aultnaslanach Viaduct*: I wish he'd made my back door frame, rotten after just 40 years! But all is not what it seems – a concrete inner viaduct was added in 2002 to take the weight off the ancient timbers.

Soon there is another more spectacular viaduct, the *Findhorn Viaduct* south of Tomatin. Built in 1894, steel trusses were used here instead of stone arches. This time the road has its own viaduct to our left (east) but the best view is right (west) down the broad valley.

After some deep rock cuttings, comes *Slochd Summit* (the sign is on our right, and you don't pronounce the 'D') – altitude just over 1,300ft or 400m, which is high – but we will go considerably higher soon. At this point we are within yards of the remains of one of the consequences of that Jacobite rebellion: General Wade's military road. Like the modern A9 and the railway, Wade had to aim for the same narrow pass.

Downhill to **Carrbridge** (milepost 90) which is signed as part of the Cairngorms National Park, and what seem to be grey clouds in the distance are actually magnificent mountains. Talking of clouds, a quite extraordinary cloudburst here in 1914 swept away several bridges in the ensuing torrents, and the line was closed for seven weeks.

Aviemore comes next and is the junction for the steam **STRATHSPEY RAILWAY** (page 181). You will see Aviemore Speyside platform on the left, but that dates from the bad old days before the steam trains were allowed back into the main station. There's also a fine signalbox and a turntable. Aviemore station proper is, looking at the buildings on the left, a fine old station with traditional canopy and lighting. The semaphore signals fit in with all this.

Kingussie, pronounced 'Kinoosie', has a large lake to the left, and a boat club for sailors with altitude. Can you get ice-breaking sailing dinghies?

Newtonmore has one platform rather devoid of population and another crowded – but only with gorse bushes. Next there is a girder viaduct running over a broad river, still the Spey, but we are shortly to turn up Glen Truim, for the Truim joins the Spey a little way further up (on our right). That we are getting high is evidenced by the old snow fences on the left. Another way of getting high is provided by the Dalwhinnie Distillery, just before **Dalwhinnie** station. On the right (west) just after it there is a dam and behind it the lengthy Loch Ericht, a hydro-electric project with a much bigger dam at the other end. More snow fences and a classic glacier-carved valley can be seen to the left.

Look out now on the right for the sign announcing *Drumochter Summit* at 1,484ft (452m). This pass is the highest point on the entire British railway system (barring weird mountain funiculars). We are in the Andes of Britain.

Now the brakes go on as we descend, which is more difficult to control than climbing. At Calvine a road takes off west towards Rannoch (loch, moor and station), which might be interesting if you have done/will be doing the West Highland Line to Mallaig. It's only about 20 miles away here, but a hell of a long way by rail.

Blair Atholl station has proper semaphore signals and a signalbox, and befitting for this aristocratic kind of place, the following bridge over the river has castellated ends. Whether this is pompous or not is not for me to say, but the Duke of Atholl who lives in the castle is the only individual in Great Britain allowed to keep a private army. It is an honourable outfit of kilted gardeners, etc, and although it marches around in fine style, has not recently fought many battles. Talking of battles, keep a lookout for when the train

PASS OF KILLIECRANKIE

BRUCE GALLOWAY

THE HIGHLAND MAIN LINE

1 The magnificent double road and rail viaduct at Findhorn 2 Pitlochry High Street 3 Teeing off at Gleneagles 4 The beautiful clock at Perth station

BRUCE GALLOWAY

LOWSUN, SHUTTERSTOCK.COM

CORNFIELD, SHUTTERSTOCK.COM

LACHLAN1, SHUTTERSTOCK.COM

slows to 30mph for the Pass of Killiecrankie, where road, rail and river must squeeze through a gap in the hills.

There are precipitous views on the right down into the river's swirling salmon pools, and a short tunnel as we screech round dramatic curves. The 1689 Battle of Killiecrankie was a forerunner of Culloden in that it was the Jacobites (supporting James II or VII of Scotland) versus the Protestants (pro-William III). The side usually called 'the English' were in fact largely Lowland Scots. On this occasion they lost, but soon won elsewhere.

Famously, a Highlander almost impossibly leapt the river here to escape the claymores of the enemy.

Pitlochry, known for its Festival Theatre, has suitably arty sculptures on the platform, plus – don't miss this superb piece of Scottish Victoriana – a wonderful cast-iron drinking fountain on the platform, fully restored in 2014. The buildings are rather lovely too, and contain a good charity bookshop, worth a browse. Next are miles of the shallow wide river on one side and the A9 road on the other, then a long girder bridge to the other bank. After a viaduct and tunnel, we reach **Dunkeld & Birnam**. If you've read *Macbeth*, you'll remember the witches' curse about Birnam Wood coming to Dunsinane comes true when the attacking army carry tree boughs to disguise their numbers, an early case of camouflage (books on that subject are naturally very hard to find). It looks like the cast-iron spandrels supporting the station canopy have been decorated by the three witches too.

The 330-yd *Kingswood Tunnel* is followed by signs of the old main line to Aberdeen trailing in from the left (this features in 'The Race to the North', mentioned on page 78, where we saw the other end of this old route).

We're now crossing fertile farmland, and if the potatoes seem behind those in the south of Britain, they are also a lot more disease-free, which is why southerners are keen to get Scottish-certified seed spuds.

Perth is a substantial station as befits the capital of Western Australia. Or Perthshire. Style: shabby mock baronial. Note the wonderful old station clock high up on the right (and an even better one on the northbound Platform 7). An equally ancient wrought-iron bridge leads across to the opposite platform where the little-used line was on my visit still held in with wooden wedges in cast-metal chairs (our own track is more modern). No need to go to a museum, then! A museum, by the way would explain that the wedges were driven in the direction of travel to counter a strange phenomenon called 'rail creep' where the rails would slowly move that way, perhaps encouraged by train brakes. Modern track doesn't.

A splendid station with far more space than Glasgow Queen Street and with, perhaps, a tenth as many passengers! In late May/June it's lupin city round here, unless someone's gone mad with the weed-killing train since.

PERTH TO GLASGOW QUEEN STREET*
STIRLING WORK
1HR 10MINS, 64 MILES

The line that joined us from the left in this station was the **TAY COAST LINE** from Dundee along the north banks of the Tay. It leaves us again after the short *Moncrieffe Tunnel* at **Hilton Junction**, with signalbox, and heads across Fife to Edinburgh via the Forth Bridge.

We cross over the Tay somewhat more easily than the line directly south from Dundee does, and speed to **Gleneagles**, a world-class hotel with its own station, and signs of an old branch platform on the right. A few years ago, the G8 world leaders including Tony Blair and George W Bush gathered here, Bush famously falling off his mountain bike after colliding with a cop sent to protect him. The 2014 Ryder Cup was also held here, to the delight of golf fans.

There's a lovely view south (left) of a glacial valley and semaphore-signalled loops. Approaching **Dunblane**, we cross two rivers. Dunblane station is a three-platform layout, with stoppers from Glasgow reversing here. The fine station building is by William Tite. The viaducts to the north and south are called Allanwater Viaduct (stone) and Kipenross Viaduct (iron) respectively. Once there was a junction here whereby trains wandered west all the way to Oban via Callender and Crianlarich (the last part being today's Oban branch). Our route onwards to Glasgow is correctly called the **CROY LINE** and has been electrified.

A tunnel is followed by **Bridge of Allan**, and views to the left of the striking Wallace Monument tower on a hill. This is roughly the hero of the film *Braveheart* (well, it's always Mel Gibson in his films) and looks like a stone space rocket. It has the most elaborate Scottish crown, festooned flamboyantly with more pinnacles than Zsa Zsa Gabor had husbands. Anyway if flamboyant means flame-like, then that's exactly what it's like. (In which case, the reader demands, how can it be a rocket with flames pointed upwards? Blast!) We cross a river with newly laid tracks to the north crossing alongside us on their own bridge, and this is the 2008-reopened **ALLOA BRANCH** (well done, Scotland, for investing in railways!).

Soon we reach **Stirling**. You can see from the circular entrance hall that it was built by the genius James Miller, whose love of curved spaces culminated in the glorious Wemyss Bay station (page 62).

After **Larbert**, a splendid triangular junction with a possible glimpse of the Falkirk Wheel (see box, page 44), we join a major east–west route (the east corner of that triangle goes to Edinburgh).

Now it's high speed through **Croy** as we make up for all that slow screeching round mountain curves back up the line. We pass **Lenzie**, **Bishopbriggs** and

SCOTLAND'S CRACKPOT RAILWAY

Isambard Kingdom Brunel famously tried the 'Atmospheric Railway', in which the train was pulled by a piston being sucked along a vacuum tube. It failed miserably. Scotland tried the opposite – a fabulously expensive attempt to blow a train along a weird overhead railway. This failed too.

Inventor George Bennie's 1930s railplane (pictured), had a cigar-shaped carriage with aircraft propellers fore and aft and was supposed to run suspended from an impossibly complicated gantry above existing railway lines. The ordinary track was supposed to carry heavy goods, while railplanes sped passengers and mail at 300mph.

Bennie paid for a demonstration line at Milngavie, near Glasgow, which opened in July 1930. The machine never reached anything like the predicted speeds, despite the great noise of thrashing the air, and World War II put paid to Bennie's dreams. Oddly, the massive rig survived until early 1956. George Bennie died the following year, aged 65, having never recovered from the blow.

Eastfield depot on the left and then past the new *Cowlairs depot* in another rail triangle. After some less than romantic housing schemes, we plunge down a tunnel to **Glasgow Queen Street**, our terminus (for comments, see page xv). You have just completed the highest main-line trip in Britain. Quite a ride!

WHISKY AND CANALS

The Great North of Scotland Railway

2HRS 20MINS, 108¾ MILES **

A vainglorious title, possibly, particularly if you realise that the 'Great North of Scotland Railway' only reached halfway, from Aberdeen to Keith. But then the English seemed to do a more ridiculous title than this, by a long chalk, with the Great Marlow Railway.

The Scots are both inordinately proud, and sometimes savagely scornful, of their railways and regiments – I mention both together because at both Inverness and Aberdeen there are wonderful war memorials worth seeing (outside and inside the stations, respectively) and also great proud memorials to the railways themselves. As related elsewhere, the railways round here were often self-financed, there not being the industry and population to draw in outside money. So they should have been, and should still be, proud of their achievements.

But you have to laugh when you read E L Ahrons on this line in 1922:

> Why it was ever allowed to be called a railway at all PASSED COMPREHENSION. As a matter of fact, part of it between Aberdeen and Inverness was not originally a railway but a canal, and the company thoughtfully scooped in the canal, baled it out, and made their line on the remains. After which some people in the district bethought themselves, when it was too late, that the canal would have been INFINITELY PREFERABLE. The stopping trains... set the pace of a glacier, only a glacier would probably have got there first.

Satirical exaggeration, but in 1880 4¼ hours got you only as far as Elgin from Aberdeen (now it's less than 1½ hours).

And the truth about that canal jibe is even funnier. O S Nock, the railway historian who quoted the above extract, goes on to tell how the original route from Kittybrewster (on the northwest side of Aberdeen) to Huntly was indeed to be built on a canal. But because the contractor couldn't be bothered to wait for the legal paperwork, he simply cut a hole through the canal bank and let the whole contents pour into the River Don. This left all the barges still in transit loaded with their cargoes and sitting on the muddy canal bottom! The outrage was such that it had to be repaired, refilled and then drained when the boats had all gone!

ODDEST ACCIDENT 1

One of the oddest railway accidents in Scotland didn't involve trains, didn't involve a railway line, nor rail staff nor passengers nor rolling stock, and there was no fatality and no person even injured. A local man drove up to a level crossing at Dunragit near Stranraer when the automatic arms came down and he stopped sharply. A following car banged into the back of him. Both drivers got out, and a pedestrian walking his dog came over to act as a witness. As they were concentrating on the car damage, none of them noticed that the train had come and gone and the crossing arm, to which the pedestrian had tied his Scottie dog's lead, had gone up… leaving the poor creature dangling out of reach. It wasn't until the next train came that the dog came down, apparently little the worse for its experience. It sounds urban myth, but examination of the original report shows names and addresses of the local people involved.

Another odd thing. When the GNoSR reached Aberdeen in 1855 it was to a separate Waterloo station, not the one you reach from the south. So you could have booked a very, very roundabout route from London Waterloo to Aberdeen Waterloo for a few years. The two Aberdeen stations weren't merged, cutting out a lot of bother for footsore travellers, until 1867.

One more funny thing: because the GNoSR was built from Aberdeen, and the joining-up railway from Inverness, the result is that the mileposts count up from both ends, so milepost 10 is at two places, miles apart, for instance.

THE ROUTE DESCRIBED

I'D SIT ON THE LEFT. This isn't one of your spectacular, awesome Highland lines. It is through lovely farmland, pleasant hills, forests, burbling rivers – lots of charm, fascinating features and beauty but no cliffhanging. And at around two hours and 20 minutes, not too long.

Inverness is a strange curved triangular stub off a line running east–west, just long enough to put the station at the bottom apex in the town centre, and a depot in the middle. The line west (left) goes to Kyle, or Wick and Thurso, and the line right goes to Aberdeen, or Perth over the mountains. So the Highland capital is also the rail hub.

PAUL TOMKINS, VISITSCOTLAND

RICHARD PAXMAN

PAUL TOMKINS, VISITSCOTLAND

JIM GRANT, SHUTTERSTOCK.COM

1 The beach at Nairn **2** Pitcaple Castle, visible on the left past Inverurie
3 Strathisla Distillery, Keith **4** Dusk falls over Elgin

Some platforms in Inverness lead left (west and north), and some right (east and south), and one short one is connected both ways. In the old days, expresses that were continuing would go past Inverness station on the Rose Street curve, and then back in so the loco was ready to take off again. How quaint, I thought – until my train from Kyle to Inverness did exactly that, because it was continuing to Aberdeen.

We turn right and probably spot a snowplough on the left. This is no anachronism. They have been needed on today's route; they are often needed on the lines to the west and north. Even at the beginning of June you can look across the waters of the Moray Firth and see snow on mountain tops. The two lines to the left of us are the **HIGHLAND MAIN LINE** south to Perth and being the wrong side, soon cross over us (right after the tunnel under the A9 road).

We get glorious views of the sea, and the Moray Firth usually manages to look cold. You may see seals on the foreshore. And is it just me, or does that house on a headland ahead left look like a stranded ocean liner from this angle?

ODDEST ACCIDENT 2

Most of us have taken a naughty swim when we weren't supposed to. A whole train did so in 1939. The story starts with a breakdown in the Haymarket Tunnel near Edinburgh Waverley. The fireman and then the driver got down to find the fault with the brakes, and eventually found a loose connecting pipe between two wagons. They put it on, only to realise the engine was still set to go, with the brakes set to pump 'off'. They hurried back to the engine as the wagons began to roll past them, but the fireman tripped over his lamp and the driver came a cropper on top of him. By the time they'd got up again the train was running away too fast to catch, with no driver up front.

They rushed to a signal telephone and called the signalman, who calculated that he couldn't let the train crash into passenger trains along the line, and couldn't let it crash into a dead-end brick wall, but could have a chance of saving it by sending it down the Granton Dock branch, luckily empty. At the back of the train was a guard's van occupied by Angus Panton, a happy man unaware of the danger. He might have been able to slow the train with his brake, and save himself too.

At the station, the signalman had organised a gaggle of people to warn Angus, and posted them halfway down the platform. They started running as the train passed and yelled: 'Ye're on the road to Granton, there's no-one on the fuitplate!' Unfortunately, they all yelled over each other, and old Angus, whose birthday it was, thought they were saying 'Hurrah for Angus Panton / Many happy returns mate!' He puffed on his pipe, smiled and waved fondly as his brake van disappeared from view. How nice of them to arrange a surprise. Which indeed it was. Only when the engine, 37 wagons and brake van went through the buffers and off the end of the dock into the water to the horror of startled dockworkers did Angus take the plunge, and save himself.

NAIRN BEACH

DVLCOM, SHUTTERSTOCK.COM

Castle Stuart, about half a mile on our left, has a Scotch crown spire, and probably flies the Saltire. Inverness Airport is close by on the right. Good farming country. An airport station, possibly called Dalcross, may be built here soon.

Next stop, **Nairn**, which had a pleasantly Ruritanian signalling system until a few years ago. There are two signalboxes, since boarded up, one at each end of the extremely long platform. Because the one signalman used to hurry from one box to the other, he was issued with a bicycle to do so more rapidly, much to the bemusement of the passengers on the train. Now they have colour light signals here and such picturesque goings-on are history.

But along this line you could see much of the old ways in railways. Under such schemes, entering single-track sections, or leaving them, the driver slows or stops to hand over to the signalman the Tyer tablet. This is a 19th-century bit of cast iron that fits in a machine at either end, a bit like putting chocolate back in a vending machine. But only the right one fits the machine. Drivers are only allowed to continue with the tablet marked for the right section – so they are legally obliged to take it out and look at it.

And this is the clever bit – the signals can't be changed without the right tablet being in the machine. Usually the train would go into a siding or trap points if it passed the red signal, but not into a head-on crash. It's a Victorian-era system. Yet it's safer than some modern systems, it's cheap and it works.

I said red signal, but much of this route is, or rather was on my last visit, manually signalled with semaphore arms. So when they stretch out straight, it means 'danger'. When they are at a slope, either up or down, they are 'off' – the equivalent of 'green'. What with jointed rails giving the old-style *clickety-clack*

147

and the telephone poles still standing alongside the track, Hitchcock could have filmed *The 39 Steps* here. There were plans afoot to modernise it all very soon afterwards, making any remarks about signalling out of date. All the more reason to go while the service was still slow!

There are beautiful views across to the mountains up the coast (possibly 20 miles away as the crow flies, more like 60 by rail!). We cross the River Findhorn on a high-sided iron viaduct.

Forres, which also used semaphore signals, was once a totally triangular station, but has now been replaced.

At 12½ miles, we reach **Elgin**, which produces not marbles but equally well-carved Walkers shortbread (the firm is based at Aberlour). Next there is a girder bridge over the wide Spey, and we enter a twisting hilly section with deep cuttings, constantly changing views and forests. This is the only section where we part company with the A96 road between the two cities for very long.

Soon we come to **Keith** and the warehouses defended by barbed wire and set carefully apart, with stringent fire precautions, just like munitions stores for the army. They are in fact bonded whisky stores. This is a spirit which is far stronger and more explosive than the stuff you can buy, so the precautions are necessary – also because tax has not yet been added to the stuff. There are sometimes thousands of barrels stored on the left here too.

Keith also has the **KEITH & DUFFTOWN RAILWAY** which runs heritage diesel railcars on a whisky-soaked branch line (page 180).

Huntly had the by now usual splitting semaphores – that is, one for each track at a loop, so you know which way you're going at the points – and therefore a signalbox too.

There's a particularly beautiful old (closed) station on the left, on a long left curve across a valley at Kennethmont. If you like a wee dram, you'll probably be looking the other way at the Ardmore Distillery, home of Teacher's whisky (and don't teachers need that stuff from time to time?).

Insch (railway museum) is described by one reader as 'a near perfect example of a former GNSR wayside station'. Now with double tracks again, and new signals, it is followed by **Inverurie**. In between there are endless old stations to spot, some overgrown, crumbling platforms, and some with residual buildings and charm, such as Pitcaple (Pitcaple Castle is on the left). You can dream about buying an old station and living amid castles and distilleries, like 1,000 others, no doubt!

Dreams, unlike drams, are free. After Inverurie a station at **Kintore** has recently been reopened. It's next to the infant River Don which we follow for most of the rest of the route. Soon, for about 10 miles, there are great sweeping meanders on our left in a particularly handsome valley.

Dyce, the next stop, is bustlingly busy, yet the nitwits in charge had it closed for some years. Now it's reopened, and adjacent to the airport and industry

ODDEST ACCIDENT 3

Another peculiar accident on the railways in Scotland also didn't involve a train, a station, any passengers, or even a railway line itself. It was an accident involving a signalbox – the one at Broomfield Road in Montrose, Angus. The signalbox was badly damaged in the collision but was not itself – of course – moving.

What happened, on the freezing cold morning of 17 October 1939, was that signalman James Clark was trying to keep warm in his lonely vigil. He descended the wooden steps to reach the coal shed under the signalman's floor, at the level where the rods and cables entered the cabin. He thus missed the shocking experience of an RAF Airspeed Oxford aircraft taking the top off his signalbox. Dumbfounded, and maybe fearing a runaway train had crashed, he rushed outside to find much of his signalbox missing and the wreckage of a plane alongside.

Miraculously, no-one was hurt in the aircraft or on the railway. World War II had started the month before, so it was necessary to try to fly aircraft in all conditions. Three planes from RAF Montrose crashed that morning, all because of heavy ice forming on their wings overnight. At this rate, the RAF 'Few' would get fewer without any help from the Germans!

Railway services were very little delayed by the 'wizard prang', as RAF slang might have it. But James Clark had had a very lucky escape.

which boomed in recent years thanks to North Sea oil (hence helicopters to land on oil rigs).

Talking about closed stations, there are now no stops between here and Aberdeen. Yet there were once seven in this populous stretch – and they wonder why road traffic is so bad in Aberdeen! Some may soon be replaced.

Anyway, there's a point down here called Kittybrewster – a name lovelier, perhaps, than the place itself. The railway that went on to the docks to the left (still there) was that original line to Waterloo, and we are on the later connector to Aberdeen Joint (as it was called). Just before we reach Aberdeen through a gloomy set of bridges and build-overs, there's a rather cute turntable pit scooped out of the rock to the right. I say cute, because their engines must have been small in those days.

And here we are at **Aberdeen**, another granite city, set between the rivers Dee and Don; an excuse to tell you a story about a lady fishing midstream in waders up the River Dee, near Balmoral. She saw another woman walking down the bank and realised it was the Queen Mother, and curtseyed correctly as she was greeted. Her waders part filled with water and the fisherwoman floated off downstream, still smiling at Her Puzzled Majesty. More about Aberdeen on page 79.

Duirinish (SUPERSTOCK)

***
2½HRS, 82 MILES

The line from Inverness to Kyle of Lochalsh, the iron road to Skye, rightly attracts superlatives. Some call it the most beautiful railway in Europe. I can understand that, although I haven't seen them all (yet). But I have spent much of my life travelling every line in Britain, however, and can swear this is among the most scenically dramatic of them all.

True, you have to want awesome mountains, rocks and rivers, jaw droppingly beautiful lochs, red deer and eagles and a journey from sea to shining sea – rather than the chocolate-box villages of thatch and cream teas of the south, so it depends what you're after. If it's wilderness and majesty and nature, this is one of Britain's best, rivalled only by the other two lines in the Highlands, plus the Settle & Carlisle.

It also has the benefit of being not too long, less than 2½ hours from Inverness to Kyle, and having a definite start and finish – the chilly North Sea to the rolling Atlantic, right across Scotland. With Inverness accessible both by overnight sleeper train from London and by plane, it's not as remote as it once was, and for whole touring trains or individuals, it's hard to beat.

Having said all that, it does have a remarkable sense of connecting somewhere to nowhere through a lot of, er, nowhere. But it has survived many perils against the odds and those locals who once resisted it being constructed now fight just as doggedly to save it. It should be up there with Stonehenge and the pyramids as an international asset to value for all time. Before describing the route (and all the towns it doesn't go through!) here's a look at its fascinating history.

FROM FEUDALISM TO INTERNET-AGE DEMOCRACY IN JUST 150 YEARS

In 1864, when locals in Inverness mooted the building of this line, the Highlands were still almost feudal. Great lairds held power over vast tracts of countryside, while their tenants and crofters lived in poverty and hardship (which is one reason why Australia, New Zealand, the United States, Canada and Hong Kong are full of people of Scottish descent. Neither were the emigrations always voluntary, with the disgraceful Clearances telling a sad tale of croft-burning and poor people being herded off the land like cattle by the rapacious landlords, who were English by legend, but in fact often Scots).

The Highlands held no great reserves of the coal or iron ore that were powering Britain's Industrial Revolution, and there were no great towns or

A BATTLE, A WAR & A HIJACK!
THE SKYE LINE'S UNBELIEVABLE SEA OF TROUBLES

The Dingwall & Skye Railway got it wrong about sea transport, which was the one thing supposed to make sense of its route through nowhere to nowhere, and then got it wronger. Its first suggested terminus which was supposed to bring in steamer-loads of passengers and goods from the Hebrides was at Attadale, but wasn't built because it was too far up shallow waters. The next terminus and pier at Strome Ferry was still so far up Loch Carron that shipping companies that took trade up and down the west-coast islands point blank refused to make the 28-mile extra journey up to Strome.

At the last minute, the railway decided it had to become a maritime power and bought two vessels to run to the islands. One was soon wrecked and the other frequently broke down. Tight-fisted local bigwigs on Skye and Lewis charged such huge rates for landing the ferries that they could never make money. A smaller paddle steamer was acquired to reduce the per-ton charge for landing on Skye. The fees were doubled, so no saving was made.

A faster, more reliable boat was eventually acquired, the *Ferret*, and the service settled into something of a pattern, with the Highland Railway taking over the shipping (and eventually the loss-making railway). Then the unbelievable happened. The *Ferret* ended up being hijacked to Australia.

It would be too far-fetched for Freddie Forsyth fiction, but it happened. To steal the Highland Railway's *Ferret*, 347 tons, 171ft long, was bizarre. She was chartered dishonestly in 1880 and 'wrecked' off Gibraltar, the railway claiming insurance on the sinking. In fact, although lifeboats and debris had been planted in the sea, she had actually been renamed and repainted.

She was put up for sale in Melbourne, Australia, but someone who knew the Highland Railway's ships (how unlikely was that!) became suspicious and alerted the authorities. In the ship's log, they found a sheet of Highland Railway notepaper and the game was up.

She was indeed sold in 1881, to reimburse the insurers, and traded legally until 1920 when she really was wrecked at Cape Spencer, South Australia. A fair way from Strome Ferry.

Meanwhile in another unbelievable episode, the Battle of Strome Pier, local west-coast fishermen who were strict Sabbath-day observers – the 'Wee Frees' – were angry at the east-coast men scooping up all the herring in the area and sending them off in the early hours of Sunday to make London's Monday fish markets.

cities to connect. The geographical obstacles were huge, the snowdrifts often deep. But men could dream, and sometimes dreamers make things happen.

This backward land could be brought directly from the 14th century to the 19th, it was argued, by building a railway through the only glens that linked directly and relatively easily across the Highlands at this level. By providing a pier at which a steamship from Skye and the Hebrides could connect with the railway, Inverness would be reachable in a few hours instead of days of struggling over rough mountain roads or dangerously round the rugged

Working on Sunday caused them great offence. On Sunday, 3 June 1883, their small boats converged on Strome Pier and took it by force, wrecking the crane. The one policeman covering the whole area was absent, and even six more sent by train from Dingwall were helpless against the mob. The protesters sang a hymn of victory and slipped away, vowing to stop trade again the next Sunday.

But the authorities were this time having none of it. A strong police detachment arrived, and 74 troops were sent from Edinburgh Castle in a special military train, held near Inverness (but the fact that it was there, and they were armed, was carefully leaked along the line). A sullen demonstration took place, but the trains were loaded with fish. The ringleaders were arrested, the police being pelted with stones by their womenfolk. They were released, feted as heroes, and life returned to normal.

Meanwhile the rival lines to Oban (page 131) and later Mallaig (page 126) were eating holes in the valuable fishing traffic. The era was known as 'the fish wars'. All three companies which had built through the Highlands with such monumental effort sent agents to the fish market at Stornoway. Sometimes they got a third of the traffic each, which went on three steamers to their respective piers, then three trains to London, but before they reached England were joined into one fish train! It was insane, or at least very illogical.

In 1897, after the government had considered various ways to assist this poverty-stricken corner of Great Britain, the subsidised extension of the railway from Strome Ferry to Kyle of Lochalsh was finally opened. It really was the iron road to Skye (nearly).

That all three of the once-rival lines to the west coast have survived is astonishing. It was seriously proposed in the 1960s that there should be no railways north of Glasgow and Edinburgh, and then it was official policy that everything should end at Inverness. The Kyle line went through the closure process in 1971 and escaped by the skin of its teeth thanks to oil exploration, which looked as if it needed freight trains to the west coast. In this sense it was saved by its biggest rival, the motor car. Now these wonderful lines are recognised worldwide for their tourist potential, bringing in special touring trains, and locally as invaluable community assets, it is unlikely they will ever be closed. But as the Skye Railway's utterly amazing history shows, anyone who even suggests such a thing will have one hell of a fight on their hands.

THE SKYE LINE

ANNIE MACDONALD

DUNCAN COGHLAN

BUCCHI FRANCESCO, SHUTTERSTOCK.COM

JOE DUNCKLEY, SHUTTERSTOCK.COM

JAMIE SQUIBBS

DALE KELLY, SHUTTERSTOCK.COM

1 At 2,975ft, Fuar Tholl is one of the most dramatic peaks on this route **2** Duncraig's unusual octagonal waiting room **3** Plockton **4** Crossing the Plantation Viaduct near Achanalt **5** Loch A' Chuilinn **6** The Skye Bridge at Kyle of Lochalsh

storm-tossed north coast. The locals in the west otherwise had to take long and sometimes perilous steamer trips to Glasgow to shop for supplies from the outside world.

The teeming fish of the west-coast lochs could find a market in England if trains reached here. Sheep would no longer lose a quarter of their weight walking to Falkirk if they could ride by train in a day. The few horses and cattle would no longer break their legs boarding steamers.

As with the other railways around Inverness, it was very much a self-build project. There was no help from outside, so this part of Scotland hauled itself up by its boot straps and joined the modern world. And outsider investors were absent, it must be said, because they could see through all this optimism that there was a virtual desert along the route, virtually no population and not a few bloody-minded landowners and no cities at the other end. All there was was lots of scenery, and would that buy tickets? No. But it would eventually *sell* them.

INVERNESS TO DINGWALL***
35MINS, 19 MILES

The building of the Dingwall–Kyle route met obstacles from the near-feudal lairds, some of whom had, after all, cleared people from the land to enjoy expensive solitude and weren't willing to change. Many of them just wanted the route altered to look better from their grand houses, and private platforms for their convenience, which they were granted.

Worse, one of them insisted that the railway at the start from **Dingwall** (on the existing line to the north) could not take the obvious route through Strathpeffer (the valley of the River Peffery), which denied it access to the only town (of the same name) on the route. This condemned it to climbing up to a summit at Raven Rock for ever more, causing no end of trouble with snow in the winter. That it was a last-minute change is shown by the way we suddenly swerve right after 2½ miles (the mileposts zeroed again at Dingwall) across the main road.

We do not rejoin it for half a dozen miles, by which time we've missed Strathpeffer, which oddly we can see clearly down in the valley on the left at 3¾ miles. Useless fact: when Strathpeffer did eventually get its branch line, now gone although the station is preserved, it was sometimes run by railway engines built for Uruguay.

For the first few miles, setting out from
INVERNESS TO DINGWALL,
read from page 163 (and it will return you here at the right spot).

The engines work hard up the steep gradient towards Raven Rock (a not-too-obvious prominence amid the forests) and a 458ft-high summit, and then the line enters a small rock cutting and emerges into a very different, more Highland landscape from the valley we left below.

We pass amid great long views of Loch Garve on our right with mountains all round. A halt comes at **Garve**, beside the loch, and here the main road which has rejoined us takes off right (northwest) to the fishing port of Ullapool (which would have been the western terminus of this line had the final approach been less steeply down). Garve station was laid out with double lines for trains to pass, and the tracks are curiously far apart. The reason was because of a plan to ship not just fish but entire fishing boats from one coast to the other when the seasons required it (thus obviating a tedious and dangerous trip around the north coast, or up the tediously diagonal Caledonian Canal). Special cranes and trucks were ordered, but like so many of the Skye line's dreams, it came to naught. It's a shame, because it deprived us of the curious sight of a fleet of fishing smacks cruising through the mountains at several hundred feet above sea level, skipper sitting on deck puffing on his pipe.

Beautiful and vast Loch Luichart soon comes on our left, and there's a ✋ **Lochluichart** halt after a hydropower station on the right (look, no pollution!). We follow the river to find two more picturesque lochs. A Chuilinn is the long wide one on our right, and then we cross to the north side of the water in this valley, Strath Bran, and Loch Achanalt is on our right, followed by ✋ **Achanalt** station. We follow the River Bran on our left, the line dead straight for a while, with the A832 road on the right keeping rail and river company, to **Achnasheen**, meaning 'field of rain' which it often is. Strath Bran has a lonely bleak beauty of emptiness. Loch Gowan, the double one on the right, is the last connected to the North Sea. There are awesome mountain views to the left and ahead.

We climb hard through bleak near-desert above the treeline to *Luib Summit*, 646ft, not marked that I could see, amid beautiful scenery of little lochs and mountains. Railwaymen were warned by locals about one of these close by on the right, Loch Sgamhain, which apparently harbours a kelpie that devours swimmers whole, leaving only their lungs to float to the surface. Nice.

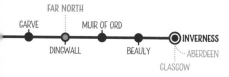

Attadale (ALEXANDER JOHNSON PHOTOGRAPHY)

By the way, if you find the landscape bleak, consider that the lengthsmen – who patrolled the line checking the joints, etc – were not provided with any accommodation or shelter for the first few years, and had to sleep under their coats, in caves and culverts, snowdrifts or not. Later there was a more paternalistic attitude evident, with the record showing a train making a weekly stop at lengthsmen's cottages so their wives could do the week's shopping in Dingwall. Wouldn't do for Paris Hilton, but better than sleeping in a cave.

Now the River Carron is often keeping us company, heading west like us, for we are in the beginnings of Glen Carron. There are impressive views of brooding 3,000ft mountains to the left.

Where we cross the infant River Carron, there was once Glencarron halt, built as a private station for the nearby Glen Carron Lodge 'for the setting down or picking up of the proprietor… or his servants'. Later, it was open to the public, who had to operate a pair of lower-quadrant semaphore signals to stop trains (which must have been fun). Mind you, the eccentric chatelaine, Lady Cobbold, was a great traveller and the first Western woman to enter Mecca (or the first to get out and tell the tale). She is buried standing up in the gardens here, facing towards Mecca. So semaphore signals must have been a doddle for her.

✋ **Achnashellach** is still open, in an increasingly pretty wooded valley with a large freshwater loch on the left, and first views dead ahead of brutal-looking Fuar Tholl, 2,975ft, and the surrounding mountains.

In October 1892, the railway suffered an embarrassing runaway here. One of its questionable mixed trains – where goods trucks were marshalled next to engines with passenger carriages at the back – was being shunted at night. Having extracted some trucks, it was necessary to nudge up to the remaining part of the train to get the coupling hook on. The trucks and carriages (holding nine passengers) began to roll back over the small summit, with engine and guard stumbling along trying to get the heavy shackle over the hook. It was hopeless.

The crew then made a bad mistake and set off into the pitch black to catch the train. Of course it had rolled up a further slope, stopped, and was now heading back towards them. The first truck was smashed to pieces, and it was a miracle that no-one was killed.

DINGWALL TO KYLE OF LOCHALSH***
2HRS 5MINS, 64 MILES

We reach wide Loch Carron soon after **Strathcarron** station, and the clear views to the right of Fuar Tholl become more and more majestic along the next few miles.

👋 **Attadale** was the original planned site for the western terminus, complete with a pier and hotel, being the first bit of salt water on Loch Carron that the cash-strapped railway reached. But it was too far up and shallow for steamers. After a rethink, Strome Ferry was decided on, and the station, pier and grand hotel to be built there instead. Except that the hotel could not be afforded, and the station was a rudimentary platform.

Attadale had a simple wooden shack in the 1950s, and a red flag was provided for 'intending passengers' to wave to stop trains. Eventually the shack blew away in a storm, taking the flag with it.

There's a good view, left, up Attadale Glen with its river, and right across the loch to the village of Lochcarron. The line now curves sharply, and has been troubled here by rock and snow falls from the early days. It even passes into an avalanche shelter. Indeed, in late 2008 a train was derailed by a landslide here, with no injuries. The frequent curves from here to the end of the line give the benefit of sweeping your window views across the magnificent outlook, and anyone who reads a book – excluding this one! – for all of this stretch should be chucked off the pier at Kyle. You can see Strome Ferry narrows ahead, for example, and through them the peaks of the Cuillins, 30 miles away on the Isle of Skye.

Strome Ferry was the original terminus, and as the name suggests, Loch Carron narrows to a few hundred yards here. The line was eventually extended to Kyle, reaching there in 1897.

There is a superb view back to the Strome narrows on the next stretch (back right, and a rather small ruined castle on the far shore), showing the dramatic way the water or rather ice cut through the mountains, and then after 👋 **Duncraig** (odd octagonal waiting room) comes **Plockton** (restaurant, loos, bunkhouse, original buildings). There's another fine view ahead right over Plockton Bay, with boats moored in it and the village beyond framed by far distant mountains. The village is so pretty that it starred in a television series, *Hamish Macbeth*.

After 👋 **Duirinish**, the long views across the sea are just fabulous. On a fine day you can see mountains up to 30 miles away, such as the Quirang, 30 miles northwest. Closer to hand the Crowlin Islands stand in the sound, about five miles away. This whole section was hewn from solid rock to make a shelf above the sea. Soon we are rattling into Kyle itself, and the trip ends at the pier and the still-substantial **Kyle of Lochalsh** station (loos, gift shop and rather good little museum). There's no need to go over the sea to Skye any more, as now there's the road bridge and a connecting bus.

Congratulations! You have finished one of the great railway journeys of the world. There's another funny thing about the Dingwall–Skye line: it's built with commendable Highland economy, with not one tunnel or great viaduct that I can recall. That's why it fits in so perfectly.

⚜11⚜
WONDERFULLY REMOTE
THE
FAR NORTH LINE

4HRS 20MINS, 167 MILES***

This is another beautiful route well worth the long ride, and very different from the west coast scenically. It is possible to go there and back in a day from Inverness, and people do, but that would be around 8 hours on trains and I'd stay somewhere at the top, fixing it in advance preferably. Or go on by ferry from Scrabster, near Thurso, to Orkney. Or start from somewhere beyond Inverness. Some of the small stops are request halts, so wave at the train when waiting at them, and tell the guard when on the train where you want to get off. In fact, it was nicknamed 'the Adventure of the 39 Stops' back in the day before many wayside halts were closed. Some have been reopened as population returned.

INVERNESS TO LAIRG***
FROM THE SLIGHTLY ORD TO THE DEEPLY LOOPY!
1HR 40MINS, 67 MILES

Leaving Inverness – and I'd sit on the right when heading north if you have a choice (in summer it's best to book) – on the west side of its railway triangle station, we cross the fast-flowing River Ness, which drains the legendary monster's lair. This bridge was swept away by floods in recent years, so the trains stuck on the two lines north of here had to carry on in splendid isolation, with buses doing the first bit.

Next we come to the **_Caledonian Canal Swing Bridge_**, protected by proper signals a decent sliding distance from the water's edge – and thus very safe – and needing a 10mph speed limit for trains (if not boats). You still get that 'bong, bong' of the wheels going over the crack. You may have seen or be going to see the similar Atlantic end on your rail touring of the Mallaig line near Fort William (page 127).

Dingwall is the junction for the **SKYE LINE** to Kyle of Lochalsh and thence Skye on the west coast (if following that, switch to page 151).

The wide inlet of the North Sea on the right is the Beauly Firth, an extension of the Moray Firth. The view of the spectacular Kessock Bridge to the Black Isle (back right) is great, although that place – one of a series of massive peninsulas divided by vast sea inlets – is neither black nor an isle. We speed on past flowering broom-lined track and gentle farmland inhabited by happy-looking cattle. No hint of Highlands yet; it could almost be Devon or Cornwall.

We cross one big river into the newish station of **Beauly**. Ahead looms the distant mass of Ben Wyvis, 3,433ft, from which summit you can see the North Sea and the Atlantic (I'm told): it usually has a lick of snow. What was that about 'like Devon and Cornwall'?

Muir of Ord is followed by another new station, **Conon Bridge**; then the spacious and original **Dingwall**, next to the Cromarty Firth. It's a Viking name: before them it was Inverpeffer. Notice 'HR' for Highland Railway on the building to the left (switch to page 135 for that line).

To start with, once the **KYLE LINE** diverges at Dingwall, the Far North Line runs through some pretty verdant and lovely countryside completely unlike the rugged Atlantic end of that other line. Foulis Castle on the left, then two distilleries. We pass through good Easter Ross farmland, gently undulating.

There is none of the wave-lashed bare rock and railway blasted out by dynamite. Perhaps this trip will be all amid gentle scenery, you wonder. **Alness** and then **Invergordon***** follow, and here the latter's strategic naval position is evident from the gap into the North Sea across the water. Nigg Bay on the right is where many North Sea oil platforms were launched (if that's the right word) and are now recovered. Sailors have to keep out of the east end of the bay, however, because of the Sands of Nigg. I love that name. 'Beware the sands of Nigg!'

At Invergordon, don't miss the brilliant murals on the Up platform (right). They are just wonderful references to this line's critical importance in two wars taking Highlanders to war, and men and particularly coal to the fleet here and on to Scapa Flow in Orkney. The unexciting

coal trains clanking through here day and night were as important as tanks on the Western Front. As David Lloyd George, Minister of Munitions, told the miners in 1915: 'Coal is everything for us, and we want more of it to win victory'. Five million tons were shipped from South Wales, much of it up here. The trains were known as 'Jellicoe's Specials' after Admiral John Rushworth Jellicoe, commander of the Grand Fleet, and there are many memorials – including at the time of writing charming little flower-bed trains on platforms – along this line.

Perfect views towards the sea follow.

The railway is in no hurry to get north; we turn west again after **Fearn** and **Tain** (at low tide you can see the 'Tain Scalps' where an unwary boat could be neaped – stuck after a particularly high tide). This is followed by two more distilleries and Skibo Castle (on the right), up the Dornoch Firth, we loop inland into Sutherland and re-emerge after 40 rail miles only ten miles up the coast. This isn't just because there are obstacles to navigate around: the railway builders deliberately took long inland loops a few times on this route to open up inland areas to rail traffic. Look how the A9 road sensibly cuts across Dornoch Firth to our right (due north).

We instead follow the convoluted Dornoch Firth to **Ardgay** and then rejoin the water (which has become the Kyle of Sutherland after a narrow bit) to **Culrain**✱✱, then the dramatic bridge to **Invershin**. By the way, in steam days the short distance from Culrain to Invershin was the shortest distance in the UK that one could travel in a proper dining car. I seriously doubt anyone would be able to sit down and bolt down even a Scotch egg in that half-mile, but if a proper restaurant car runs, I'll give it a go. Now we climb up a steep gradient across more highland country following – of course given the last station name – the River Shin with fine views left (south) and reach **Lairg**, which is well inland. The railway swung this far inland intending to tap into the rural hinterland, as the village stands at the head of the inland Loch Shin and thus is the junction of a whole set of Highland roads to remote places.

The railway was used for taking out great trains of sheep, fish, stone, timber and whisky and bringing in oil, coal, newspapers, tools and tourists with dozens of specials laid on for seasonal demand. O S Nock's book tells of five special sheep trains leaving Lairg in less than 24 hours; today there are none.

Then fleets of buses met the locals and tourists. Today, if you're lucky, a handful of people get off the admittedly faster and more frequent trains, and no staff meet them; one wonders if the 30-mile diversion from a more direct route is still worth it. There have been rumblings about building a rail bridge at Dornoch to cut out this inland stretch and speed up the long journey north.

THE FAR NORTH LINE

SUPERSTOCK

STEVEN T. WALDSCHMIDT

ROB FAULKNER

SUPERSTOCK

Photo credits: STUART CROY, GILL KENNETT, SHUTTERSTOCK.COM, JOHN K PERRY, CLAUDINE VAN MASSENHOVE, SHUTTERSTOCK.COM

1 Brora **2** The wonderful murals of Invergordon station **3** Altnabreac is one of the few stations in the UK without any road access! **4** The end of the line: the aim of most visitors to Thurso is to reach John o'Groats **5** Dornoch Firth **6** Wick Harbour **7** Forsinard station **8** Helmsdale

DUNROBIN CASTLE

SORIN COLAC, SHUTTERSTOCK.COM

LAIRG TO WICK & THURSO***

MIDNIGHT TRAIN TO GEORGEMAS!

3HRS 40MINS, 104 MILES

I take the view that one has come to see the scenery, not to hurry, and this route gives such great variety. The special trains today are touring trains. The timetable is more intense in the summer and trains lengthened. Anyway, it's not all gloom on the freight side. Timber and stone trains have been seen again on this route, some of it marble bound for Italy via the Channel Tunnel, which makes it a coals-to-Newcastle story if there ever was one, and a pretty long train ride. It is amazing that this line was built, and amazing that it has survived. Looking out of the window at sea, valleys and mountains (or should that be straths and bens?), it still is amazing. And startling that once or twice one is briefly heading slightly south when going north!

Indeed, after climbing steeply to *Lairg Summit*, we descend southeast along a suitable valley (the river of the Fleet, as if to make visiting journalists feel at home). We pass through **Rogart***, heading (oddly) slightly south and a lot east. Rogart was piled high with smelly wreckage one winter's night about 100 years ago when 22 wagons broke away from a fish train and ran back (continuous brakes on wagons not then being compulsory). The quick-thinking signalman at Rogart heard them coming and threw the points to divert them into a siding instead of smashing into the following passenger train waiting at the station. No-one was killed, but a lot of herring were damaged in the mountain of wreckage.

Soon we see on the right an embankment called The Mound, which the great highway engineer Thomas Telford threw across here in 1815 (like The Mound in Edinburgh) and brings the A9 road back beside us. In fact, a branch line from here south to Dornoch once used the same embankment.

Now we see the North Sea proper. Through **Golspie**, and then **Dunrobin Castle** – the fairy-tale historic castle is glimpsed to the right overlooking the North Sea as we pass through what was the Duke of Sutherland's private station of the same name (a rather nice half-timbered building which looks like an aristocrat's play-house, which it sort of was). In fact, the line building had stopped short at Golspie because money ran out, until the duke saved the project.

After **Brora**** (followed by a bridge over the river of the same name, a distillery, and the spot where the last wolf in Scotland was killed in 1700) we and the A9 follow the coast – you might see seals, cormorants, herons and oystercatchers – until **Helmsdale****, where we turn sharply inland yet again even though Wick is only 30 miles up the coast. We follow the picturesque River Helmsdale in its flat-bottomed valley on our right for miles – this is Strath Ullie. We climb through increasingly bleak countryside, through **Kildonan** (scene of a short gold rush in 1868) and **Kinbrace**.

We pass close to Loch An Ruathair on the left, and the remote halt of **Forsinard**** (the village is nearly a mile further up the road north). The stop is nicknamed Frozenhard by rail staff when drifting snow fills in the gap level with the platforms! The name in fact tells a story because the first part is Norse (Viking) for waterfall – as in High Force in County Durham – and indeed means much the same, as the second part is Gaelic for 'high place'. No English here, chummy!

This is the seriously bleak Flow Country, and we climb over empty Caithness moorland to the line's County March summit at 708ft, on the shoulder of a hill, 3.9 miles after Forsinard. (Before you write in, I know there's an intermediate summit of the same name on the West Highland – in fact do write in and explain it if you can!)

There have often been snow fences built up here, and not without cause – passengers have sometimes been marooned on trains for days with only a humorous guard to keep them sane until rescued, and, in at least one case on one of these Highland lines, by an Arctic Snow Cat, a tracked vehicle more usually seen in polar regions, which could climb over the snowdrifts.

As for the route, I think we can discount the earlier excuse that the railway was trying to open up the interior population – there isn't any! – and in fact was trying to get north as cheaply as possible without ruinously expensive bridges and tunnels. I like the swooping S-bends that result near the summit, as long as it doesn't snow too much.

There are odd halts such as ✋ Altnabreac* (a request stop we slow for but probably don't halt at – it has no road to it!). There is little visible except miles of conifer plantations and peat bog, great for birdlife, not for nightlife. On the right, the River Thurso rushes through the landscape and, then, under the train.

Eventually we descend through **Scotscalder** into flat country and a

> ## EVEN FARTHER
>
> 'I rescued the most obscure railway in the British Isles from oblivion by writing a little article about it for *Railway Magazine* when I was 16. On Unst, the most northerly of the Shetland Islands, I found some overgrown tracks of a tiny 2-foot gauge running from chromite quarries in the island centre to a nearby pier. Stocky little ponies were pulling ramshackle wagons full of chrome-iron ore in the hot July sunshine... I felt I had reached the ultima Thule of the railway world.'
>
> Eric Lomax, *The Railway Man*

settlement is reached at **Georgemas Junction**. The train can go straight on for 14 miles to **Wick**, a pleasant run past Loch Watten, or reverse left seven miles, still with the A9 road, to **Thurso**. It chooses reverse first. It's slightly bonkers that people going to Wick see Georgemas Junction twice in 20 minutes, but locals have got used to it. Four times if you are going back today!

The reason for this odd layout is that this Wick/Thurso line got here first, and it's not worth having a train stationed at the junction to shuttle the last few miles (as in the old days). Neither town is large, but the sense of place is magical.

Georgemas Junction has a useful and used freight terminal on the right, bringing in pipes for North Sea work, taking out nuclear waste from the old power station at Dounreay, and maybe the recently announced nearby spaceport will need this somewhat less rocket-speed means of transport to get materials in. A nuclear flask train left going south when we were popping up to Thurso. What a long ride to Cumbria!

Thurso – the name means 'Thor's River', so close are we to Viking homelands – has hotels, and a pleasant walk west along the cliffs to Scrabster (also served by bus from the station, handy for connecting with the Orkney ferry). On that walk is not only a useful supermarket on the left but also tantalising views of Orkney, if it is clear, and nearer, on the right of the bay, the cliffs of Dunnet Head. This is an RSPB reserve, and the most northerly point of the British mainland. It has a lighthouse on that side to help mariners across the Pentland Firth, where the whirlpools and overfalls of water reveal how the swirling cold waters of the North Sea and the Atlantic struggle and collide.

The real aim for some people is the last village in the British mainland, John o'Groats, easily reached by bus or taxi if you are staying. You might reasonably think there are no British railways north of here, and you are right. But there were at least a staggering 33 on Orkney, nearly all military, quarry or docks railways. There was one you could ride on, run by the eccentric composer, Sir Peter Maxwell Davies. There was even one more on Shetland, further north – found by one of my heroes, Eric Lomax (see box, opposite). Read the first chapter of his wonderful book *The Railway Man* (which is about war, not railways, and was made into a film with Colin Firth and Nicole Kidman) to learn more.

And if you look at the buffer stops at Thurso station clearly one naughty loco did get a centimetre or two further north by walloping them so that they are bent!

But the truth is you have reached the most northerly proper passenger station in Thurso, and the exhibits here tell something of the history and the Jellicoe Express. In fact, if you want history, go outside on the platform and look at the 'chairs', the cast steel things holding the rails on the sleepers. You will soon find the initials 'LMS' – which means this track is older than 1948!

Well done with your adventuring. You have crossed unique landscape to reach a rail extreme point. There's nowhere remotely like it.

THE END OF THE LINE: THURSO

ROMANCE & RIVALRY ON THE RAILS

SCOTLAND'S RAILWAYS in MOVIES, BOOKS & POEMS

POETIC RAILS

I recently came across this lovely poem by A M Harbord. It's about something I noted in my earlier book, *Britain From the Rails* – how London Paddington somehow contains the coves of Cornwall, how Liverpool Street has the wide-open Norfolk broads and eastern fens within it. And nowhere is it more true than with Scotland. Euston and King's Cross contain the lochs, the glens and straths, the mountains, the lowland cities and highland towns. Perhaps I'm nuts, but I liked this. It seems to be written in about 1925 about someone wistfully remembering trips to Portree (on Skye, but reached by train then, as now, to Kyle of Lochalsh).

Stranger with the pile of luggage
Proudly labelled for **PORTREE**
how I wish, this night of August
I were you and you were me!

Think of all that lies before you
when the train goes sliding forth.
And the lines athwart the sunset
lead you swiftly to the **NORTH**.

Think of breakfast at Kingussie
think of high **DRUMOCHTER PASS**.
Think of Highland breezes singing
through the bracken and the grass.

Scabious blue and yellow daisy
tender fern beside the train
ROWDY TUMMEL, falling brawling,
seen and lost and glimpsed again

You will pass my **GOLDEN ROADWAY**
of the days of long ago.
Will you realise the magic of the
names I used to know:

Clachnaharry, Achnashellach,
Achnasheen and Duirinish?
Every **MOOR** alive with covers,
Every pool aboil with fish.

Every well remembered vista more
exciting mile by mile
Till the **WHEELING GULLS** are screaming
round the engine at The Kyle.

Think of cloud in Bheinn na Cailleach,
jagged Cuillins soaring high.
Scent of peat and all the **GLAMOUR**
of the misty Isle of Skye!

Rods and **GUNCASE** in the carriage   Go, and **GOOD LUCK** travel with you!
wise retriever in the van;   (Wish I'd half your luck, my man!)

LITERARY GIANTS ON THE RIGHT LINES

The greatest poem about a Scottish railway is, oddly enough, about a train that no passenger ever travelled on, and started in the wrong country. It is also, some believe, the greatest film about Scottish railways too.

Written and produced in 1936, *Night Mail* was a documentary effort as public relations for the General Post Office, and as a morale-booster for its staff. This short two-minute black-and-white film – which can be easily found on YouTube – happened to employ, for mere promotional purposes, a truly great poet and a truly great composer: W H Auden and Benjamin Britten. It concerns a type of train now extinct: the travelling post office.

Of course in those days, and up until not many years ago, almost every train carried a few mail bags in the guard's compartments, dropped off at sleepy country halts for a postal van to pick up. Travelling post offices (TPOs) were something different. They had sacks of raw Scottish mail (in this case) loaded at London Euston, which were then sorted overnight into the walks postmen would use in the morning delivery. This meant – amazingly really – that a postal worker who lived in, say, Harrow, north London, would not only work overnight in alternating directions, but would know intimately the geography of – for example – Elgin and Nairn. Which street was on which walk, which farm was where.

It was before postcodes made this simpler, and before emails made most of it unnecessary. And of course the TPOs have long gone, as are the steam engines that pulled them, the postmen who ran them, and various details like

A TRAVELLING POST OFFICE IN *NIGHT MAIL*

the ingenious hooks and nets that would allow hanging sacks of mail to be safely dropped off from a speeding train or picked up from the wayside by a non-stop express roaring past.

One more intriguing detail about the film – one shot shows the postmen sorting letters at frames inside the swaying train. This just couldn't be done in the dark, narrow railway carriages with the cameras of the day. So a postal frame was built in a studio in London, but real postmen were called upon to act the part. Then they realised they had to show some sort of sway to make it look real. So they put the whole thing on a platform that swayed. The result made test viewers feel sea-sick. They then tried swaying the camera while the postmen stayed put. The result was jerky and ridiculous. In the end they resorted to a bit of string, while both the sorting frame and camera stayed still. The string moved left and right and the postmen keeping it in the corner of their eyes swayed with it. At last it looked real!

What's so good about Auden's poem – and it's best to read it first, then watch the film – is how the verse mimics the beat of the steam engine, and where speed increases, the rhyme doubles in speed too (by being internal in each line). The italic bits are simply spoken prose, but still – to my mind – great use of English.

This is the **NIGHT MAIL** crossing
the Border,
Bringing the cheque and the postal order,
Letters for the rich, letters for the poor,
The shop at the corner, the girl next door.
Pulling up Beattock, a steady climb:
The gradient's against her, but she's on time.
Past cotton-grass and moorland boulder
Shovelling **WHITE STEAM** over
her shoulder,
Snorting noisily as she passes
Silent miles of wind-bent grasses.
Birds turn their heads as she approaches,
Stare from bushes at her blank-faced coaches.
Sheep-dogs cannot turn her course;
They slumber on with paws across.
In the farm she passes no one wakes,
But a jug in a bedroom gently shakes.

Dawn freshens. Her climb is done.
Down towards **GLASGOW** *she descends,*

Towards the steam tugs yelping down a glade
of cranes
Towards the fields of apparatus, the furnaces
Set on the dark plain like gigantic
CHESSMEN.
All Scotland waits for her:
In dark glens, beside pale-green lochs
Men long for news.

Letters of thanks, letters from banks,
Letters of joy from girl and boy,
Receipted bills and invitations
To inspect new stock or to visit relations,
And applications for situations,
And timid lovers' declarations,
And gossip, gossip from all the nations,
News circumstantial, news financial,
Letters with holiday snaps to enlarge in,
Letters with faces scrawled on the margin,
Letters from uncles, cousins, and aunts,
Letters to Scotland from the South of France,

Letters of condolence to Highlands and Lowlands
Written on paper of **EVERY HUE**,
The pink, the violet, the white and the blue,
The chatty, the catty, the boring, the adoring,
The cold and official and the heart's outpouring.
Clever, stupid, short and long,
The typed and the printed
and the spelt **ALL WRONG**.

Thousands are still asleep,
Dreaming of terrifying monsters

Or of friendly tea beside the band in
Cranston's or Crawford's
Asleep in working Glasgow, asleep in well-set
Edinburgh,
Asleep in granite Aberdeen,
They continue their **DREAMS**,
But shall wake soon and hope for letters,
And none will hear the postman's knock
Without a quickening of the heart,
For who can bear to feel himself forgotten?

Rivalry among the railways was fierce when they ran parallel routes. The Caledonian and the competing Glasgow and South-Western used to run competing services before the 1923 grouping forced them together, and drivers were seen shaken their fists at drivers of the other trains where they ran parallel, roaring through stations at hair-raising speeds to get to junctions first, and indeed blaming each other when there were accidents. A glimpse of the spirit of those days is illustrated in the last verse of this poem by the driver of the Sou-West's train 259.

We left St Enoch station, our time was **EIGHT-SIXTEEN**.
The electric light was shining: her beauty there was seen
We ran our miles so **SPEEDILY** and reached Dumfries at time,
And we beat the Caledonian with the Two-Five-Nine!

DREAMS OF THE SUBLIME, RHYMES OF THE RIDICULOUS

One of the most underappreciated railwaymen poets in the world is Scotland's Alexander Anderson, who wrote as 'Surfaceman' (his job with the Glasgow and South-Western, a trackworker) in the late 19th century. Completely self-educated, his style was accessible and still is. In his work *The Wires*, he recalls a lunchbreak dozing on a hot day on the grassy embankment looking up at those telegraph wires, which for passengers used to rise and dip by the carriage windows (before the internet and all that – the first world wide web was telegraph, youngsters!). He fantasises about what messages they are carrying. It starts:

I lay beneath the long slim wires,
And heard them murmur like desires

And then he dreams of what the nine wires are carrying, glad or sad tidings, one by one. This long, dreamy reverie comes to an abrupt, rather comic end, bringing him back to business:

The voices CEASED, and half dreaming still | 'What can the BURDEN be of its rhyme
In the drowsy shade of the slope, I thought | When it speaks?' and I had not long to wait
'Eight wires have murmr'd their good or ill | 'Limited mail is sharp at her time
There are nine, but the ninth has spoken not. | But the Pullman is twenty minutes late.'

William Topaz McGonagall of Dundee, mentioned in the section on the Tay Bridge disaster (see box, page 69), gets rightly derided as the world's worst poet for applying the above technique to that event so crassly. It's not worth reprinting except as entertainment. It starts – and remember he'd just written a poem praising the bridge as the 'Beautiful Railway Bridge of the Silv'ry Tay!'

After the disaster he wrote:

Alas! I am very SORRY to say
That ninety lives have been taken away
On the last SABBATH day of 1879,
Which will be remember'd for a very long time.

… and then gets worse.

What is not widely known is that there is a longish and quite touching poem by the 19th-century German poet, novelist and travel writer Theodor Fontane (very popular at the time) about this event – *Die Brück am Tay*. Reader Dr Gordon L Mackenthun kindly wrote to explain 'Fontane's artistic trick is to bring in the three witches from Macbeth (in the German version the Shakespeare quotation is in English too). And he constructs a family drama with the "bridge people" waiting for their son who is on the doomed train.' I have had a read of the translated work… and, well, it's better than McGonagall.

A MYSTERY IN THE MOUNTAINS

Back to the first theme in this chapter for the last entry. I don't know who this was written by. It was left pinned to the door in the Ryvoan bothy – a shack-like shelter for walkers, a life-saver in dire weather – during World War II. This bothy is about 3 hours' walk east of Aviemore station, in the Cairngorm Mountains, but don't try to find it without proper maps, guides and equipment. Some say it was written by a lady from Cumbria who had loved the area as a child.

What I do know is that walkers have been careful to make sure a copy of the poem has stayed there for the past 80 years. The first four lines are:

I shall leave tonight from Euston
By the seven-thirty train,
And from Perth in the early morning
I shall see the hills again.

And the poem ends after reminiscing about the glories of the mountains and glens:

And again in the dusk of evening.
I shall find once more alone
The DARK WATER of the Green Loch,
And the pass beyond Ryvoan.

For tonight I leave for Euston.
And leave the world behind:
Who has the hills as a lover,
Will find them WONDROUS kind.

FURTHER READING

Le Vay, Benedict *Britain from the Rails: A Window Gazer's Guide* Bradt, 2019. Now where's my own trumpet? Time to blow it! The precursor of this volume, this book met with great success over several editions. It wasn't just government ministers and industry leaders who praised it (seriously), but endless readers gave it enthusiastic five-star reviews that really counted. There is some limited overlap with this book, but I hope you'll forgive me.

Ransom, P J G *Iron Road: The Railway in Scotland* Birlinn, 2010. Thoroughly recommended history going right back to the 18th century – a nicely produced, attractively illustrated book. My copy didn't quite come up to the present day but it doesn't matter – we know about that and this, brilliantly, is a first-class look at what went before.

Spaven, David *The Railway Atlas of Scotland: Two Hundred Years of History in Maps* Birlinn, 2018. This is an extraordinary, eccentric book that you can't quite believe any publisher took on but you are glad that they did. It isn't an atlas and not of railways that you can use, in the usual sense of those words. It is a collection of old maps of sidings, maps of railways that were never built or have long gone, but nothing laid out like a road atlas. And no use for taking as a guide – mind you, you'd need a lectern to rest the huge thing on. But totally fascinating if you like maps and railways history. Brilliant coffee-table browser.

Thomas, David St John and Whitehouse, Patrick *The Romance of Scotland's Railways*. Out of print but you can always find bargain copies of this lovely hardback. Anything on railways by David St John Thomas is worth reading – he was the publishing pioneer who set up David & Charles because big publishers turned their noses up at books about trains (and other enthusiasts of specialist subjects). It was a life-long success.

STEAMY AFFAIRS

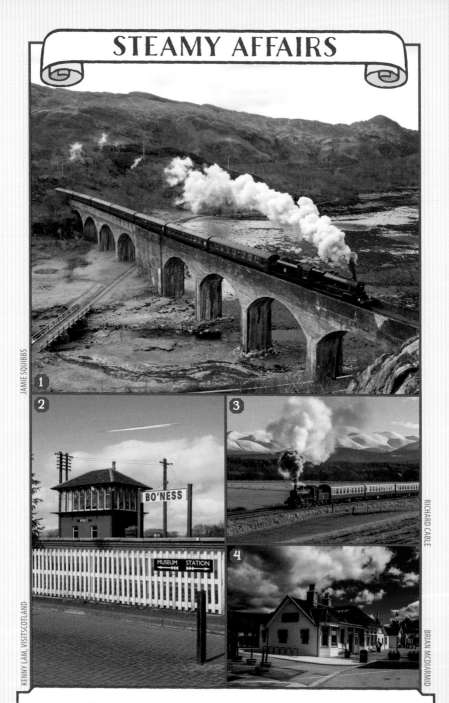

JAMIE SQUIBBS

KENNY LAM, VISITSCOTLAND

RICHARD CABLE

BRIAN MCDIARMID

1 The *Jacobite* crosses the viaduct at Loch Nan Uamh **2** Bo'ness station on the Bo'ness and Kinneil Railway **3** The Strathspey Railway at Boat of Garten **4** Ballater station was carefully rebuilt after a fire in 2015

Steamy Affairs

A SELECTION OF SCOTLAND'S WONDERFULLY VARIED COLLECTION OF STEAM & PRESERVED RAILWAYS

Climb on board the Nostalgia Express – first stop, transport history. Trips range from the long and luxury to the short and industrial. We have done our best to get the details right but things change over time, so please check before travelling to a venue.

STEAM RAILWAYS
BO'NESS & KINNEIL RAILWAY
BKRAILWAY.CO.UK

This fascinating medium-sized heritage railway runs in Bo'ness, variously described as in the Central Lowlands, or West Lothian, or Falkirk district. It's on the south bank of the Firth of Forth about 3 miles north of Linlithgow. It is run by the Scottish Railway Preservation Society (SRPS), and operates a total of over 5 miles of track (between Bo'ness and Manuel Junction, via Kinneil and Birkhill). Three stations and a small halt, plus a growing stable of steam locos and a really impressive collection of historic rolling stock makes this a serious concern. It may form the nucleus of a larger railway museum in the future. Unfortunately, services do not connect directly to the railway system (perhaps because it's such a busy high-speed main line where the branch joins). Travel to Linlithgow, thence by bus from outside the Four Marys pub.

CALEDONIAN RAILWAY
CALEDONIANRAILWAY.COM

With the atmosphere of a lovely old country branch railway, this operates (mostly at weekends) heritage steam and diesel-hauled trains along the 4-mile line between the town of Brechin and the countryside stop of Bridge of Dun. Brechin is off the A90 Dundee–Aberdeen road, about 25 miles out of Dundee. Rail to Montrose, then bus to Brechin.

DOON VALLEY RAILWAY
DOONVALLEYRAILWAY.CO.UK

Previously called the Scottish Industrial Railway Centre, Dunaskin, this group aims to mark the key role railways played in the massive industrial past of this area south of Glasgow. To quote them directly: 'Our aim is to preserve and operate those small and versatile industrial steam and diesel locomotives – known to generations of Scots as 'Pugs' – in a similar environment to the one in which they spent their working lives.' These are not the glamorous passenger express locos which achieved fame, but hardworking little engines with four or six wheels, typically. Visitors can ride passenger trains through the countryside, and also examine the far-ranging collection of steam and diesel locomotives, including their unique working 'Fireless' locomotive built by local firm Andrew Barclay, Sons & Co Ltd of Kilmarnock – a type which was necessary in munitions stores, for example, or mines liable to gas infiltration, or for handling certain flammable or explosive materials – has now been restored to full working order. Check on open days before travelling. There is a regular bus service, number 52, from Ayr.

FIFE HERITAGE RAILWAY
FIFEHERITAGERAILWAY.CO.UK

Run by the Kingdom of Fife Railway Preservation Society at Levenmouth, Fife, this has half a mile of track and the USP – unique steaming point, as it were – is that all the preserved locos spent their working lives within about 20 miles of here. So the emphasis is on small industrial locos, steam or diesel, typically four-wheelers. If this group keeps going until the main line reaches back to them, which is happening, this little operation could be more of a success. Until then, the best option is by road.

THE *JACOBITE*
WESTCOASTRAILWAYS.CO.UK/JACOBITE/STEAM-TRAIN-TRIP

Scotland's – and Britain's – most successful steam operation, running proper trains over proper railways (the real network, not a private line) at proper speed. And not just any proper railway – one of the world's most beautiful lines, from Fort William to Mallaig, including the globally famous Glenfinnan Viaduct which has starred in movies. Sensational, not be missed! For more details, see page 122.

KEITH & DUFFTOWN RAILWAY
KEITH-DUFFTOWN-RAILWAY.CO.UK

The K&DR is Britain's most northerly heritage railway and its past – and sometimes present! – is steeped in whisky, still a major employer around here.

Their station, Keith Town, is a little walk from the main line one, but if you are hurrying through the streets, they say they'll hold the train if you call them. That's real country railways for you! Keith is on the Aberdeen–Inverness Line (page 143), or the A96 if you're arriving by road.

THE ROYAL DEESIDE RAILWAY
DEESIDE-RAILWAY.CO.UK

Travel in the tracks of Queen Victoria as she trundled down the branch towards Balmoral. This line, originally from Aberdeen to Ballater, was built between 1853 and 1856 by the Deeside Railway Company and closed by British Railways in 1966. A small portion – about a mile – has reopened from Milton of Crathes station, and very pleasant it is too, in lovely countryside. You can see Crathes Castle, and the route also runs close to the Dee, which rises in the Cairngorms and gives Aberdeen its name. It's all rather charming, as are the volunteers who serve a good afternoon tea. Ballater, by the way, had a lovely old station with royal waiting room, a bit like the one at Wolferton near Sandringham in Norfolk, England. Sadly it burned down in 2016, although a careful rebuild has restored the buildings and its chintzy tea rooms; but note it is a replica, and served by no trains (so far!). Not connected to the railway system, on the A93 about 10 miles southwest of Aberdeen.

THE STRATHSPEY RAILWAY
STRATHSPEYRAILWAY.CO.UK

One of the best in Scotland, a proper, mainly steam, railway operation running 10 miles from Aviemore, Highland and connecting with Network Rail at that station, to Broomhill via Boat of Garten. The real McCoy with signal arm clanking up, doors slamming, waving green flag, Acme Thunderer whistle blowing, steam hissing, *clickety-clack* on the track – and fine dining is a possibility too. Set amid fab scenery – the weather to be negotiated on the day! Main-line station: Aviemore.

STEAM MUSEUMS
GLASGOW MUSEUM OF TRANSPORT
POINTHOUSE PL, GLASGOW G3 8RS

Scottish main-line locos, sailing vessels, trams, classic cars, vintage lorries and motor buses are all on show at this exhibition at the Riverside Museum. There was also a 'Fireless' steam loco the last time I looked (see opposite). Thoroughly worthy of a whole afternoon, and free. Striking main building, with zany zig-zag zinc roof, is by famed architect Zaha Hadid. Nearest station:

Partick or Exhibition Centre, both on the Argyle Line reached in less than 10 minutes from Glasgow Central, both stations requiring a 15-minute walk. More details: page 35.

LATHALMOND RAILWAY MUSEUM
M90 COMMERCE PARK, LATHALMOND, DUNFERMLINE KY12 0SJ
🖱 SHED47.ORG

This is about preserving part of the once-huge military/industrial railway complex in Fife. Based in the original World War II locomotive shed, dating from 1942, at Royal Naval Stores and Transit Depot Lathalmond, the Shed47 Railway Restoration Group has, over the last 23 years, been recreating some of the vast internal railway network that existed here until 1971. You can see standard gauge and narrow gauge, as well as four locos that came from the Navy docks complex at Rosyth. Some of the coaches are loaned from the Scottish Railway Preservation Society (SRPS) across the water at Bo'ness. Within the grounds of the Scottish Vintage Bus Museum, with which it makes a brilliant shared visit on its opening days (limited, Sundays mainly, so do check). Public transport not available to site – take a taxi from Dunfermline Town station.

STEAM HOLIDAYS
RAILBOOKERS
☎ 020 3780 2222 🖱 RAILBOOKERS.CO.UK

This London-based travel agency specialises in independent rail travel, with a wide range of imaginative trips and great tours suggested, including Scotland, without, as they say, all the booking and researching hassle.

RAILWAY TOURING COMPANY
☎ 01553 661500 🖱 RAILWAYTOURING.NET

This UK-based operation offers all-inclusive rail holidays to Scotland (as well as the rest of the UK and Europe), as well as terrific steam day trips and luxury tours.

SEND US YOUR SNAPS!

We'd love to follow your adventures using our *Scotland from the Rails* guide – why not tag us in your photos and stories on Twitter (🐦 @BradtGuides) and Instagram (📷 @bradtguides)?

NOTES

INDEX

W

waggonway 1
Wallace, William 48
Wallyford 27
Waterman, Pete 25
WCML 6, 32–8, 49
Wemyss Bay Line 58–62
West Calder 52
West Coast Main Line *see* WCML
West Highland Line 115–31

West Kilbride 96
Wester Hailes 49
Whitecraigs 55
Wick 170
Williamwood 55
Winchburgh Junction and Tunnel 46
Woodhall 104

Y

York 19–20

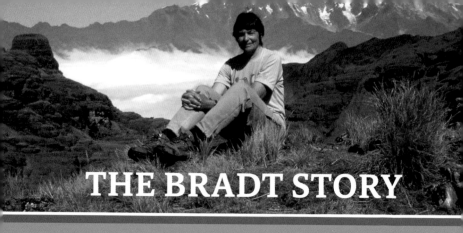

THE BRADT STORY

In the beginning

It all began in 1974 on an Amazon river barge. During an 18-month trip through South America, two adventurous young backpackers – Hilary Bradt and her then husband, George – decided to write about the hiking trails they had discovered through the Andes. *Backpacking Along Ancient Ways in Peru and Bolivia* included the very first descriptions of the Inca Trail. It was the start of a colourful journey to becoming one of the best-loved travel publishers in the world; you can read the full story on our website (bradtguides. com/ourstory).

Getting there first

Hilary quickly gained a reputation for being a true travel pioneer, and in the 1980s she started to focus on guides to places overlooked by other publishers. The Bradt Guides list became a roll call of guidebook 'firsts'. We published the first guide to Madagascar, followed by Mauritius, Czechoslovakia and Vietnam. The 1990s saw the beginning of our extensive coverage of Africa: Tanzania, Uganda, South Africa, and Eritrea. Later, post-conflict guides became a feature: Rwanda, Mozambique, Angola, and Sierra Leone, as well as the first standalone guides to the Baltic States following the fall of the Iron Curtain, and the first post-war guides to Bosnia, Kosovo and Albania.

Comprehensive – and with a conscience

Today, we are the world's largest independently owned travel publisher, with more than 200 titles. However, our ethos remains unchanged. Hilary is still keenly involved, and **we still get there first**: two-thirds of Bradt guides have no direct competition.

But we don't just get there first. Our guides are also known for being **more comprehensive** than any other series. We avoid templates and tick-lists. Each guide is a one-of-a-kind expression of an expert author's interests, knowledge and enthusiasm for telling it how it really is.

And a commitment to wildlife, conservation and respect for local communities has always been at the heart of our books. Bradt Guides was **championing sustainable travel** before any other guidebook publisher. We even have a series dedicated to Slow Travel in the UK, award-winning books that explore the country with a passion and depth you'll find nowhere else.

Thank you!

We can only do what we do because of the support of readers like you – people who value less-obvious experiences, less-visited places and a more thoughtful approach to travel. Those who, like us, take travel seriously.

TRAVEL TAKEN SERIOUSLY